A PARENT'S GUIDE TO A SAFER
CHILDBIRTH

EXPECTING THE BEST: USING THE POWER OF KNOWLEDGE TO HELP YOU DELIVER A HEALTHY BABY

GINA C. MUNDY

Copyright © 2023 by MUNDY, LLC

A Parent's Guide to a Safer Childbirth: Expecting the Best: Using the Power of Knowledge to Help You Deliver a Healthy Baby

All rights reserved. No part of this publication may be reproduced, distributed or transmitted in any form or by any means, including photocopying, recording, or other electronic or mechanical methods, without the prior written permission of the publisher, except in the case of brief quotations embodied in critical reviews and certain other noncommercial uses permitted by copyright law.

Although the author and publisher have made every effort to ensure that the information in this book was correct at press time, the author and publisher do not assume and hereby disclaim any liability to any party for any loss, damage, or disruption caused by errors or omissions, whether such errors or omissions result from negligence, accident, or any other cause.

Adherence to all applicable laws and regulations, including international, federal, state, and local governing professional licensing, business practices, advertising, and all other aspects of doing business in the US, Canada, or any other jurisdiction, is the sole responsibility of the reader and consumer.

Neither the author nor the publisher assumes any responsibility or liability whatsoever on behalf of the consumer or reader of this material. Any perceived slight of any individual or organization is purely unintentional.

The resources in this book are provided for informational purposes only and should not be used to replace the specialized training and professional judgment of a health care or mental health care professional.

Neither the author nor the publisher can be held responsible for the use of the information provided within this book. Please always consult a trained professional before making any decision regarding treatment of yourself or others.

The following pages contain true stories regarding legal cases involving labor and delivery and testimonies from witnesses, including expert witness testimony. In some cases, the specific details and names have been changed or omitted to protect their privacy.

ISBN: 979-8-88759-987-8 - paperback

ISBN: 979-8-88759-988-5 - ebook

ISBN: 979-8-89109-035-4 - hardcover

I have written this book for my children, Abigail, Elliana, and Liam, as well as for everyone dear to me. Among them is Angie, who holds a special place in my heart and is like a daughter to me. One day, may this book serve as a guiding light for all of you as you embark on the beautiful journey of childbirth.

Please visit ginamundy.com for more information on this book, author, and how the power of knowledge can help you deliver a healthy baby.

Dear Reader:

For over two decades, my career has been focused on analyzing mistakes made during labor and delivery when lawsuits have been filed against doctors, nurses, midwives, and hospitals. Drawing from this unique experience as an attorney and as the mother of three children, I have written this book to help expecting parents avoid mistakes made during childbirth. Unlike conventional pregnancy books that may focus on breathing and relaxation techniques, this one was written to provide a deeper understanding of the importance of the decisions made during childbirth.

Through the power of knowledge, you can make better decisions as you navigate the journey of childbirth. By understanding different aspects of labor and delivery, being aware of the common mistakes, and recognizing the importance of each decision made during this transformative process, you hold the key to a positive birth experience. The power of knowledge will help you embrace your intuition, heighten your awareness, and make good choices for you and your precious baby.

Remember, you are not alone on this journey. Countless hours of research, years of experience, and the wisdom gained from analyzing every aspect of labor and delivery have been distilled into these pages. My mission is to share what I have learned so expecting moms have the information they need to make decisions in the best interest of themselves and their babies. I want to stress that this information is not intended to dictate your choices during labor and delivery, but rather to empower you with the knowledge needed to make informed decisions. As a mother, these are the insights I would share with my children.

While this book provides helpful information, it is essential to understand that there are different perspectives on childbirth, and this is just one of them. It is also important to keep in mind that attorneys bring a distinct viewpoint, as we are trained to assess risks and strive for the best possible outcome based on our knowledge and experience.

While my profession revolves around labor and delivery, I am neither a doctor, a nurse, nor a licensed medical professional. The information provided in this book is NOT intended to provide medical advice. It should be used as a guide along with other resources and your own personal knowledge about labor and delivery. Ultimately, my hope is that you will use the knowledge presented to help bring your understanding of labor and delivery full circle, so you can make well-informed decisions on one of the most significant days of your life.

Gina Mundy

Table of Contents

Introduction: The Born Emergency 9

Chapter 1: Knowledge Is Power: The Lessons 19

Chapter 2: Foundation of Labor and Delivery 39

Chapter 3: The Dream Team: The Role of Your
Delivery Team 53

Chapter 4: How to Choose "The Good Doctor" 73

Chapter 5: Best Hospital for Baby 95

Chapter 6: Do I Need a Labor and Delivery Plan? 105

Chapter 7: The Baby Advocate .119

Chapter 8: Monitoring Your Baby during Labor:
The Gold Standard 131

Chapter 9: What You Need to Know about Your Baby's
Heart Rate during Labor 141

Chapter 10: Tests to Evaluate Baby's Well-Being and
Interventions during Labor 167

Chapter 11: Learning from the Legal Baby Cases to Avoid
Future Mistakes 179

Chapter 12: Are Epidurals Safe in Labor? 199

Chapter 13: Understanding the C-Section Option before and during Labor 207

Chapter 14: Pitocin in Labor 219

Chapter 15: A Perfect Gift from God 245

Additional Resources and Information 249

Acknowledgments 251

About the Author. 257

Index 259

Introduction

The Born Emergency

My phone rang at 5:30 on Friday evening. I answered with excitement, expecting to hear the good news that my niece Sam had her baby. Instead, it was one of those moments that you will never forget where you were. I was standing in my kitchen surrounded by my kids, anxiously waiting to hear about Cousin Sam.

I answered my phone, and in the middle of my typical long, drawn-out, "Heeeeey," was my sister, Sam's mother, hysterically crying. She just kept repeating, "The baby crashed, the baby crashed." I ran outside, away from my kids, so they could not hear their aunt Kelly. In her broken voice, she told me they had rushed Sam out of labor and delivery to the operating room to do an emergency cesarean section. The baby's heart rate had abruptly dropped and was not coming back up.

This was the scenario in many legal baby cases when a mistake was made; they typically end with an emergency C-section. The families from the cases rely on the delivery team to guide them and help safely deliver their baby. When a mistake occurs or the team misses something, the claim is that they did not deliver the baby in time. Having scrutinized years' worth of such cases, I had become all too familiar with the frantic chaos that engulfs the labor and delivery room as the delivery team races against time to deliver a healthy infant. It was at that moment that I could not help but wonder if the same heart-wrenching scenario that frequently played out in legal baby cases was now unfolding during Sam's labor and delivery.

As I listened to my sister crying over the phone, I sat outside silently, staring at the ground. In my head, I went from legal analysis to human analysis. I started thinking of all the families I had talked to over the years in my baby cases—the tears pouring from their eyes when they relived the day their baby was born. I understood how these families felt for the first time in all these years. It brings a feeling of helplessness as you realize that no decision now will change the past. All you can do is hope and pray that your baby will be okay.

As I continued to sit on the phone listening to my sister sob, I started to replay everything that had happened in the past 24 hours. Sam had already been lucky and made life-changing decisions to get her where she was that day.

I went back to the first phone call on Thursday night, March 17th. My sister called me to say Sam was not feeling well. She was 38 weeks pregnant and had been sick for the past couple of days. She was dehydrated, tired, and not feeling well from the stomach flu. My sister was calling to ask me whether I thought Sam should go to an IV lounge to hydrate versus going to the hospital for an IV. My niece had been sick a couple of times that winter, so she was trying to avoid being around sick people during the last weeks of pregnancy. While I could understand the rationale behind the question, through my eyes, there was a more critical issue. I explained to my sister that they needed to go to the hospital for one primary reason: they could check on the baby and make sure she was doing okay. Mom and baby are connected, so if the mom is not doing well, it is essential to ensure her baby is.

Sam headed to a small local emergency room and got her IV, but they did nothing to check on the baby. She asked the nurse if they had a fetal monitor to check her baby's heart rate and see how she was doing. Your baby is inside you, and the only way they can talk to you is through their heart rate *(see Chapter 2)*. However, this was a small local emergency room with no fetal monitors.

Sam asked another critical question that we would later learn would ultimately change the course of the night, her pregnancy, and her life: "Where can I go to have my baby checked out?" She explained to the nurse that she mainly came to the emergency room to have her baby put on a fetal monitor. The nurse contacted another hospital where Sam could have the baby checked and let them know she was on her way.

Approximately 45 minutes later, Sam arrived at the hospital. She went to the triage area, and they started the fetal monitor. The nurses and doctors were immediately concerned about her baby's heart rate. They did some further testing with an ultrasound, which was also concerning. The doctors and nurses advised Sam that they wanted to admit her to labor and delivery.

Now that it was time for the baby to come, it was decision time. They offered Sam a C-section or an induction with Pitocin to deliver vaginally. Sam wanted a vaginal delivery, which meant a Pitocin induction.

It was now 2:50 in the morning, and my phone was going crazy. "Gina, are you awake? Sam has been admitted to the hospital, and they are concerned about the baby."

"Are you awake?"

My phone was on "do not disturb," and I was asleep. Minutes later, a loud sound came through my room and startled me. The noise was like a *whoosh*, and my heart was racing when I woke up. I looked over and asked my husband what that noise was, but he was sound asleep. While lying in bed wondering about the sound, I looked over, and my phone lit up for a brief second; another text from my sister said, "Please, call me."

I called my sister, who was at the hospital with Sam. She told me that the delivery team was concerned about the baby and that they were inducing Sam. I was concerned about the plan; to be frank, I did not like it. I explained, "If the baby is not doing well, then she will likely have a hard time during labor."

Labor is tough on babies. Contractions squeeze the baby and temporarily decrease their oxygen. While this is a normal part of labor and babies are made to handle contractions,

The Born Emergency

they may not be able to handle the stress of contractions if they are already struggling.

I continued to explain that there are so many unknowns, as the baby is inside Sam and cannot be physically assessed or examined. The baby's lifeline is the umbilical cord and the placenta; even the condition of those is not known until delivery. In Sam's case, we knew the baby was struggling inside for some reason, but no one knew why. Following the analysis to my sister, I told her the baby did not need any more stress, and if Sam had a C-section, she would be holding her baby in about 30 minutes.

That morning, I could not figure out if my sister had poor communication skills or if my niece was being stubborn, but she wanted no part of a C-section. With no other choice in sight, I shifted gears from the C-section to the thought of a Pitocin induction. This was hard; I am not a fan of Pitocin. It is the most common factor in legal baby cases. When I get a new baby case at the firm, the first words I typically read are, "Mom is being induced with Pitocin." Through my legal eyes, I had seen the bad outcomes from Pitocin since my first case in February 2003. The only good news was that the lessons I had learned from Pitocin inductions gone wrong would now help me prepare my family.

I designated my sister as the baby advocate. She was responsible for ensuring the baby was doing okay during the induction. The first step was a crash course on reading the baby's heart rate. This would be key during the induction. If the baby was not tolerating the contractions, it would be clearly demonstrated in her heart rate (*see Chapter 9*). Next, she was to oversee the contractions and ensure the baby had adequate time to rest and recover before being squeezed again by the next contraction.

Then I explained that since this is a Pitocin induction and the baby already had a concerning heart rate, it is imperative that the most accurate and reliable fetal monitor be used to watch the baby's heart rate and contractions. I explained the difference between an internal monitor that attaches to the baby's head and an external monitor that is placed on the mom's belly. An internal monitor is the more accurate method and should be placed as soon as possible *(see Chapter 8)*.

Next, I told her to ask the nurse to tell her every time she increased Pitocin and to keep track of how much Pitocin was running through the IV. It is easy to do; they usually start at one milliunit and go to twenty milliunits. The nurse will increase it by one or two milliunits every time, which can be every 30 minutes or so. The nurse should make sure Sam is comfortable with the increase. If the contractions were adequate and Sam was dilating, there was no reason to increase it. In many legal baby cases, it is the higher Pitocin dosages that can lead to problems for the mom and her baby.

My next question for my sister: "Do you like Sam's delivery team?"

The team at the hospital was excellent and very well-liked by my niece and the family. After the delivery, Sam would tell me, "I loved my nurse, Caila." That is important; the families

The Born Emergency

in legal baby cases often relay unpleasant experiences with their nurse or doctor. You should get a warm fuzzy feeling from your delivery team, and you should trust them. They are the most important part of your labor and delivery. They will help guide you and bring your baby safely into this world.

Throughout the morning and afternoon of March 18th, I received videos and text messages of the baby's heart rate. It was okay, but it had dropped a few times. Everyone was watching it very closely, and they kept the Pitocin dose low to avoid stressing the baby more than they had to. There were more conversations about Sam having a C-section. However, Sam wanted to push forward with vaginal delivery, and the doctors were okay with continuing the induction. I was on edge; everyone was on edge. We just wanted the baby to be here safely. She would be the firstborn in the next generation of our family.

Then, just like that, I was back at the 5:30 p.m. phone call that landed me outside on my porch. I was still listening to my sister cry as we anxiously waited to hear about the baby. Then a glimpse of hope, as I could hear a nurse coming into the room to talk to my sister. They put me on speakerphone as my very upset sister announced she was talking to her attorney, who was a baby lawyer. While I rolled my eyes and shook my head back and forth, I could hear the calm voice of the nurse. She explained that the baby's heart rate improved in the operating room, and the new plan was to use forceps to help deliver the baby. My sister asked me if it was a good plan, and I reiterated what the delivery team already knew: the baby needed to be delivered as soon as possible. The nurse left the room and would come back after the baby was born.

My sister stopped crying; it was the hope we had been praying for—a sigh of relief that I can never explain with words. We said our goodbyes, as there were other calls to make. My sister would call me back after she knew more about the baby. I went back into the house as my kids stared quietly at me. My daughter finally asked, "Is everything okay with Sam?"

I responded, "I think so, but we all need to pray." After waiting some time, we finally got that call; our baby girl was going to be fine. Today, she is a healthy and happy little girl.

This experience was a close call that scared me and my family. Though we were fortunate that it ended with a healthy baby girl, I have witnessed the other side of close far too many times in legal baby cases. These are the heart-wrenching stories where families were just one decision or a few minutes away from a healthy baby, only to find themselves on the wrong side of a close call due to a mistake or oversight during childbirth.

On March 18th, while I tried my best to give my family important information over the phone, it was too late in the game. I was 1100 miles away from Sam that day. The realization that I may not be around for the birth of my grandchildren set in. I knew it was time to write down what I had learned from the last two decades of analyzing legal baby cases. Once I switched gears from attorney to author with the purpose of helping families have the safest possible labor and delivery, it became apparent that there was much more to learn from these cases than I could have imagined. Finally, this book was born.

Chapter 1

Knowledge Is Power: The Lessons

When you are holding your baby for the first time, you are holding more than just a new life—you are holding *your* life, and your family's life. You are at the beginning of a journey, a new chapter of life that will forever be a part of you. The first time you get to see their eyes and little fingers, as you imagine what your future holds and all the memories you will build together—their first words, first step, first smile, or the first time they look into your eyes—it is in that instant you realize you can no longer picture your life without them.

The stories in this book are a reminder that labor and delivery is one of the most important times not only in your life, but your family's life. The ripple effect of delivering a healthy baby is life-changing, forever, because you never stop being a parent. While you may transition into the role of a daughter's or son's best friend when they become an adult, you will always be their parent, always the wise one who helps guide them through life. You are holding your future, your family, your life in that powerful moment when you hold your baby for the first time.

As you prepare to welcome your little one into the world, some stories in this book may be difficult to digest. But remember: *knowledge is power.* Within these pages lies the power to comprehend how something as miraculous as childbirth can also profoundly impact your life. The power to know that it is not good enough to just roll up to the hospital in labor and hope for the best, because that is how each of these stories starts. The power to realize that, armed with this knowledge, you can now prepare yourself in ways that families could not in the past. You now have the power to learn from the experiences of other families. This knowledge is the key to navigating your childbirth with clarity. It is the power that will allow you to approach this pivotal moment in your life with both humility and strength, and emerge from it with a deeper understanding of the incredible power of knowledge.

As you explore the pages of this book, you may find yourself experiencing a range of emotions—tears, laughter, and perhaps a touch of nervousness. But let me reassure you: these feelings are all perfectly normal for any expectant parent. For just as you would go to great lengths to prepare your child for the challenges of adulthood, it is equally important to prepare for their arrival into this world. This book is not just a collection of stories—it is a powerful tool that will equip you with the information and insights you need to navigate the journey of childbirth. So, embrace the emotions that may arise, and use them as a catalyst to fuel your desire for knowledge and preparation. For in doing so, you are taking the first step toward becoming the best parent you can be and giving your child the best possible start in life.

The stories, the cases, the experiences, and the technical knowledge—it is all here for you to learn as you get ready for that powerful moment when you hold your baby for the first time.

The Lessons

In a legal case involving a baby, an attorney can only speak privately with witnesses on their side of the case. Since my witnesses were the delivery team, I could have multiple private conversations with them throughout the case. However, as I was not the attorney for the family, I could only talk to them through a "deposition," which was one chance to talk to the mom, dad, and other family members about what they believe went wrong during labor and delivery. These depositions were lengthy, lasting for hours on end, as families shared their experiences during childbirth. They were emotionally draining and always difficult stories to hear.

When it was time for the deposition of the people on the delivery team, preparing them was just as challenging as listening to the families. This is because when something goes wrong during labor and delivery, it affects everyone involved. Tears were shed frequently behind closed doors during my meetings with the delivery team.

Following the testimony of the family and the delivery team were the depositions of the expert witnesses. Each case had multiple experts hired to analyze the care the mom and her baby received during childbirth. The experts hired by the family focused on the mistakes made during labor and what should have been done so that a healthy baby could have been born. The experts hired by the hospital would testify in support of the delivery team and explain why the care provided was reasonable.

In analyzing the conversations with the family, delivery team, and experts, there are valuable lessons to be learned. We can glean positive insights from these negative experiences that can help prevent future mistakes. This chapter presents these lessons that were derived from examining all sides of the equation. Each lesson, whether from the perspective of the family, delivery team, or experts, offers insights that can help achieve the ultimate goal of ensuring the birth of a healthy baby. In the following chapters, we will dive deeper into each of these lessons, providing detailed information to help you apply them effectively to your labor and delivery.

Lesson #1 Learning about Labor and Delivery

In the world of legal baby cases, it is common for families to fall into the same trap that we all do—believing that bad things only happen to other people. However, this mentality can be dangerous, as it leaves you vulnerable on one of the most important days of your life. It is crucial to prepare yourself and understand labor and delivery. Unfortunately, for many families, this understanding comes too late, as they learn about childbirth only in the aftermath of something going wrong. They begin to piece together what happened and what could have been done differently. By gaining a deeper knowledge of labor and delivery before experiencing it firsthand, you can arm yourself with the tools necessary to make informed decisions and protect the health and well-being of both you and your baby.

When learning about labor and delivery, it is essential to begin by grasping the basic terminology and concepts. Not only will this help you make good decisions, but the ripple effect is just as important. For instance, by knowing the basics, you can communicate more effectively with the delivery team. It prevents unnecessary explanations from distracting you from the important information you need to know. This streamlined communication ensures that everyone is on the same page during your labor and delivery.

Chapter 2 of this book is dedicated to giving you a simple and straightforward version of the basics. This includes key terms and concepts that I frequently use when analyzing a legal baby case or discussing labor and delivery with a mother.

Lesson #2 The Delivery Team

In legal baby cases, the quality of care provided by the delivery team is the central focus of the case, with their actions or inactions being analyzed more than any other part of the case. Similarly, during the day of your delivery, your team is one of the most critical aspects of your birthing experience.

They will provide guidance and support throughout the process to help you safely deliver your precious little one.

Keep in mind that your delivery team is made up of humans. As humans, making mistakes is in our DNA. While doctors and the people on your delivery team try hard every day to keep their patients safe, mistakes happen. An expert doctor in a legal case gave a good explanation as to how mistakes can happen during labor and delivery.

> None of us are perfect. The bottom line is that every one of us is capable of making errors and mistakes in our lives. We do it all the time … I'm not disparaging the doctor in any way to say he's a horrible, hurtful physician. He just did the wrong thing on that particular day that resulted in a significant injury to this infant, which is a lifetime injury, unfortunately. It's the same way great drivers go through red lights, because he wasn't paying attention properly. This is what happens once in a while. It's the same thing that happened in this particular case. (*Expert Witness*)

The key takeaway from this testimony is that you need to make sure your delivery team is engaged and paying close attention to you. In the "Born Emergency," my sister was convinced that the delivery team paid extra close attention to Sam because I was on the phone telling her what questions to ask. Whether it was reviewing the baby's heart rate or wanting to know how much Pitocin was running, my sister kept the team engaged with these questions. Not only was she talking their language, but she also did it in a way that built a good rapport with the delivery team. She was nice, kind, and knowledgeable. In response, she felt that the team paid extra close attention to not only Sam, but to her.

To prepare for meeting your delivery team, it is essential to have a solid understanding of what to expect and what to look for. In Chapter 3 of this book, you will find valuable information to help you effectively assess your delivery team. From understanding how I analyze a delivery team in a case to learning how to use your heart and brain together to evaluate your team, this chapter covers it all. You will gain insight into each team member's different roles and responsibilities, what questions to ask, and what to expect during your labor and delivery. Though this chapter may require a little extra effort and attention to detail, it is undoubtedly one of the most important ones in the book. By taking the time to read and absorb the information, you will be well-equipped to evaluate and work with your delivery team effectively.

Lesson #3 The Good Doctor

From the conversations that occur behind closed doors with doctors to the public testimony in legal baby cases, one thing is crystal clear—doctors do not agree when it comes to childbirth. It was very common to talk to two different doctors and get two very different opinions about the care a mom received during childbirth. Each doctor would be adamant that they are right, and the other was crazy. There was no meeting in the middle or understanding of where the other doctor was coming from. The most intriguing aspect of this is that, at times, these doctors worked at the same hospital.

What this disagreement means to you is simple. One doctor may make a recommendation and another doctor may have a completely different opinion. These are recommendations that could be made before or during labor and become very important to you, as they will likely influence your decisions. These decisions are crucial during labor. When good decisions are made, good things happen, including the safe delivery of a healthy baby.

It is important to pick the right doctor for you. Just like there are many types of patients, there are many types of doctors. The good news is that you have some great doctors to choose from. My experience in the field has taken me across the country more than once, meeting different doctors. From the experts to fact witnesses, I have traveled to almost every state, hashing out labor and deliveries with countless doctors. While some may irritate me, I found the majority are caring physicians trying to do their best for their patients. They understand that a mistake in their world is unlike a mistake in any other profession.

In Chapter 4 of this book, I share my expertise in selecting a doctor that is right for you. Drawing from my experiences with doctors such as the "Yoda Imposter" and the

"Doctor at Trial," this chapter covers everything you need to know about picking the right doctor for you and your baby.

Lesson #4 Know Your Hospital

Selecting the appropriate hospital for delivering your baby is of utmost importance, particularly when you have a more high-risk delivery. In such cases, it may be wise to choose the hospital first, even before your doctor. This is because your doctor can only deliver your baby at a hospital where they have privileges. If you select a doctor first, you will be restricted to delivering your baby at the hospital where your doctor has privileges, which might not be the most suitable option for you and your baby's well-being.

The hospital you choose may be more critical than your delivery team, as they can only operate within the resources available at the hospital. How fast a baby can be delivered depends on which hospital you are delivering at. Smaller community hospitals may not be adequately staffed to deliver your baby quickly, especially at night when hospitals tend to have less staff. This may cause delays in decision-making and even longer waits before delivering your baby, putting your baby's health at risk.

Another critical factor to consider when choosing a hospital is the level of after-birth care your baby will receive. Different hospitals provide varying levels of care, with some offering specialized teams of doctors to help your baby if they require special attention at birth. If you opt for a smaller hospital with minimal care and your baby needs specialized care, they will have to be transferred to another hospital (sometimes by helicopter), resulting in downtime during transport where they may not receive the necessary support. Plus, you will have to deal with the emotional impact of your baby leaving the hospital where you are a patient.

Chapter 5 of this book provides a comprehensive guide to selecting the right hospital for the delivery of your baby. It covers various factors to consider, such as hospital levels and the importance of knowing the hospitals around you.

Lesson #5 Have a Labor and Delivery (LAD) Plan

While all the preparation in the world cannot fully prepare you for the experience of labor, making an LAD plan will help you significantly. As the contractions start and your body responds to the intense pain, you may feel a whirlwind of emotions, from fear and uncertainty to excitement and anticipation. While it is completely normal to feel this way, it is important to remember that you have an important role to play in making decisions that will help bring your baby safely into this world.

This is where an LAD plan can be incredibly valuable. By creating a detailed plan ahead of time, you can be better prepared to handle the unexpected twists and turns of labor. If something changes rapidly during labor, you can stay focused and make informed decisions regardless of how you may be feeling at that moment.

When I am preparing for a long cross-examination of an expert witness in a legal baby case, it requires meticulous planning and organization. That is why I always write down my strategy, plan, and questions, and review it a few times to ensure I am fully prepared. During the actual cross-examination, there is simply no time to reference my notes, but the act of preparation helps me to be mentally sharp and ready for anything that may come up. Just like in labor, these cross-examinations do not always go according to plan, but being well-prepared allows me to pivot and adapt quickly to any unexpected challenges.

Similarly, by having a clear idea of your preferences, you can enter labor knowing that you are ready to face whatever comes your way. In Chapter 6 of this book, you will find an essential guide to preparing your LAD plan. Other books may refer to this as a birth plan; both have the same benefit, which is getting you ready for childbirth. This chapter will provide you with valuable insights to help you get ready for the big day.

Lesson #6 Have a Baby Advocate

Having a supportive and trusted family member or friend designated as your "baby advocate" can make all the difference during labor and delivery. This person is responsible for monitoring your baby's well-being and helping you make informed decisions when presented with multiple options by your delivery team.

In the story of "The Born Emergency," Kelly serves as Sam's baby advocate. With her experience of delivering five children naturally and her excitement to meet her first grandchild, Kelly was an excellent advocate for Sam during labor and delivery. Although she did not have any medical training, she kept the delivery team engaged, asked thoughtful questions, and acted as a liaison between Sam and her delivery team when necessary.

Rather than simply having family or friends present at the hospital, designating someone as the baby advocate gives them a specific role and responsibility. Chapter 7 will dive deeper into the importance of having a baby advocate, with a powerful story that highlights the significance of this role. It will also provide guidance on how to prepare this person to be a good advocate during your labor and delivery.

Lesson #7 Know the Types of Fetal Monitors

In the "Born Emergency," Sam's delivery team used an internal monitor to assess the baby's heart rate and the contraction pattern. This was smart as there were concerns about the baby and they were inducing her labor with Pitocin. An internal monitor is the most accurate way to assess the baby's heart rate and contractions. The other types of fetal monitors do not accurately measure the strength of contractions and are not as precise as an internal monitor.

In legal baby cases, when the wrong fetal monitor was used, it has caused a significant delay in the delivery of infants. Most of the time, this delay resulted in the infant passing away before or after birth. For this reason alone, every parent must be aware of the different types of monitors and the pros and cons of each, all of which are discussed in Chapter 8.

Lesson #8 Know What Your Baby's Heart Rate Means

Understanding and interpreting your baby's heart rate is not rocket science, but it seems like the medical community wants to leave the interpretation of it to the medical professionals. I have studied babies' heart rates as a nonmedical person and can tell if a baby is a rock star or struggling during labor. This is good stuff for parents to know during labor and delivery. It will shed light on what the delivery team is saying if there are any concerns about the baby's heart rate and will help parents make the important decisions during childbirth.

In the "Born Emergency" story, Sam's knowledge and understanding of the importance of monitoring her baby's heart rate proved to be crucial. When she arrived at the second hospital, the nurse immediately placed the fetal monitor on Sam, and it quickly became apparent that her baby was struggling. Though the exact cause was unknown at that moment, the fact that they were aware of the issue with the baby's heart rate allowed the delivery team to help Sam create a plan to deliver her baby safely.

Chapter 9 of this book is an essential resource for any expecting parent. It provides crucial technical knowledge on interpreting your baby's heart rate during labor, which can help you make informed decisions about your baby's health and well-being. While the chapter may require some effort and time to comprehend fully, the benefits of understanding your baby's heart rate cannot be overstated. Therefore, I encourage you to take the time to read this chapter carefully and spend at least an hour or two learning about your baby's heart rate. If you do this, you will be able to understand your baby's heart rate, empowering you to make informed decisions during labor and delivery.

Lesson #9 Understanding Tests and Interventions in Labor

During labor and delivery, if your delivery team has concerns about your baby, they will perform tests or start an intervention to help improve the oxygen to your baby. They do not go straight from concern to C-section. Instead, there is a process that must be followed when your baby's health is at risk. The process typically starts with concerns about your baby's heart rate. Next, the delivery team responds to the concerns by doing tests and interventions. If baby's condition improves, they may suggest continuing with the current plan. If baby's condition is not improving, they will likely recommend a different plan.

In Chapter 10, you will learn what these tests and interventions mean for your little one. The results of both can impact your decisions during labor and delivery, so understanding them before labor starts will help you make good decisions. Furthermore, these tests and interventions are done frequently in baby cases, and the important lessons covered in this chapter will help guide you if these are performed during your labor.

Lesson #10 Common Facts and Issues in Legal Baby Cases

There are common facts and issues in legal baby cases that every parent should understand. If you know these issues and facts, and they occur in your labor and delivery, you will have a heightened sense of awareness to help make sure these mistakes do not happen in your labor. Let us take the example of a drug called Pitocin, which is used to induce labor by stimulating contractions. It is by far the number-one most common factor in legal baby cases. While this drug may scare a baby lawyer like me, doctors seem fine with it and use it all the time. If your doctor recommends Pitocin to induce your labor and you agree, now you know that Pitocin and mistakes can go hand in hand. To combat this, you need to understand what a Pitocin induction is and what is important to know during a Pitocin induction. The combination of preparation and your heightened awareness of Pitocin and mistakes will help you make more careful decisions, thus avoiding these mistakes.

It is completely normal to feel nervous if a common fact or issue in a legal baby case arises during your labor. In fact, being nervous can be a good thing, as it can help activate your intuition. Ignorance may seem like bliss, but it is not recommended on one of the most important days of your life. Your body's natural reaction to nervousness is to keep you safe, and it can help guide you when your brain perceives something to be important. When you are nervous, you are more alert and less likely to let your guard down.

When I prepare a fact witness for a deposition, the best ones are nervous. They always think that since they are so nervous, they will be a bad witness or screw up the case. My response is always the same: a nervous witness is the best witness. Being nervous always made the witness more focused and alert during their deposition. They listen carefully to each question before responding. They are always more prepared and have a better understanding of the case. They keep their guard up and avoid saying something stupid. There are many reasons why being nervous is a good thing, so embrace it and know that your mind and body have got your back.

Chapter 11 of this book contains crucial information regarding the common issues and facts related to baby cases. By reading this chapter, not only will you gain a deeper understanding of these issues and facts, but it will help activate your intuition to protect you and your baby.

Lesson #11 Safety and Epidurals

Many mothers choose to have an epidural during labor and delivery, as it can provide pain relief and make the birthing experience more comfortable. The lesson is that while epidurals are very common, it is a medical procedure that carries risks. After a very sad case where a mom passed away after receiving an epidural, I never looked at them the same way. The hardest part is that the family still does not know how their mom passed away. It was the most difficult part of my job, the struggle between being human and the confidentiality associated with being the attorney for the hospital. Witnessing the pain and suffering of a family who was left without answers, and being unable to give them the closure they needed, has always weighed heavily on me as a mom, wife, and human being. While I have pondered the thought of gathering news clippings to form an anonymous letter to the family, while I wear thick gloves so my fingerprints never touch the paper, this is not an option. What I can do is try my best to make sure that this never happens again. That is why Chapter 12 of this book is so important. It provides valuable information on how to help you have a safe epidural experience.

Lesson #12 Understanding C-Sections

In legal cases involving babies, it is worth noting that most of them ultimately result in a C-section delivery. When complications arise during labor and delivery, it can be the fastest way to deliver the baby depending on the labor.

That being said, it is crucial for expectant mothers to be aware of the potential need for a C-section and to understand what it entails. That is where Chapter 13 of the book comes in. This chapter is dedicated to providing valuable insights and information about C-sections, so you can make an informed decision if your delivery team presents this procedure as an option.

Lesson #13 Pitocin Is the Most Common Fact in Legal Baby Cases

Pitocin is the most common factor in legal baby cases. Whether it was used improperly, administered incorrectly, or caused a complication, the majority of legal cases involve Pitocin.

It is important that expectant mothers educate themselves on the potential risks associated with Pitocin, particularly if there is any chance that you will receive it during labor. In Chapter 14, you will learn many facts about Pitocin that are discussed in the legal baby world. You will learn that delivery teams run their inductions differently depending on the hospital. The chapter also provides a guide to help moms have a safe Pitocin induction, which was created based upon the lessons learned from the legal baby cases.

Decision-Maker: Why Learning the Lessons Is Important

You hold the ultimate decision-making power as the person going through labor and delivery. Your delivery team acts as trusted medical advisors, guiding you through the process and helping you make informed decisions. However, they cannot make decisions for you without your consent. Any medical procedure or medication, including Pitocin, a C-section, an epidural, or an IV, requires your approval and consent.

It can be helpful to think of yourself as a general in a battle, a company CEO, or a rock band manager. Leaders in these positions have gained knowledge and experience before becoming decision-makers. Their knowledge allows them to make the right decision when necessary to keep their soldiers safe, their company profitable, or to find the next big deal for the rock band. Similarly, you are in charge of your labor and delivery, and while you may not have prior experience, you can educate yourself to make informed decisions that result in the safe delivery of your baby.

It is hard to make good decisions if you do not know all the facts. Without educating yourself, it is challenging to determine what is good or bad care or whom to trust. The power of knowledge will help you discern what constitutes good care and guide you on whom to trust. As you read and learn, you will have the necessary tools to ask good questions and confidently be proactive in your labor to make sure you are making the right decisions.

Good decisions can be life-changing, as demonstrated in the story of the "Born Emergency." Sam's decision to ask a critical question at the first hospital likely changed the course of her pregnancy and possibly her life. She proactively asked the nurse, "Where can I go to get my baby checked out?" when the hospital was about to send her home without ensuring her baby's well-being. Sam knew having her baby's heart rate checked on the fetal monitor that night was crucial, so she made the decision to ask. Less than 24 hours later, she was holding her healthy baby girl.

By educating yourself and absorbing the insights outlined in this book, you can equip yourself with the knowledge necessary to make informed decisions. Much like Sam, this knowledge can be instrumental in helping you achieve the ultimate goal—a healthy baby.

Chapter 2
Foundation of Labor and Delivery

I still remember the day, 7,348 days ago, when I had my first big telephone conference as a brand-new attorney. I was tasked with discussing a complex legal baby case with an out-of-state doctor who was an expert in the field. As the phone rang, my heart raced with excitement and nerves. When the doctor answered, I confidently introduced myself and began throwing around legal jargon like I knew what I was talking about. But as we started to talk about the medical aspects of the case, my confidence quickly evaporated. My pen could not keep up with the doctor's rapid-fire explanations, and I found myself stumbling over unfamiliar terms and concepts. Panic set in as I realized how little I actually knew about labor and delivery. Looking back, that phone call taught me a valuable lesson: basically, I knew nothing about labor and delivery.

With over two decades of experience in the field, I now have a better understanding of labor and delivery. However, that phone call continues to linger in my memory. I recall feeling very overwhelmed during the conversation. I cannot help but wonder how much easier it would have been had I possessed a little more knowledge about labor and delivery that day. If only I had known a few key things, I would have started my day on a better note instead of wanting to rip the phone out of the wall to end the conversation prematurely. Nevertheless, I have come to terms with this experience, as it has inspired me to write this chapter. By sharing my insights, I hope to provide you with essential information I wish I had known 7,348 days ago.

My goal in this chapter is to provide a short and sweet overview of labor and delivery, particularly the aspects I find important when analyzing a legal case or speaking with a mom about labor and delivery. By doing so, I hope to offer a simple yet informative guide on the basics of childbirth.

#1 There Are Two Patients

The experts always start off by separating the patients. A doctor has two patients when caring for a mom in labor: the mom and her baby. In the obstetrical field, the mom is the first patient, and the baby is the second. Therefore, in almost all cases, the mom is the priority patient, and the baby is a close second.

A mom is also a more accessible patient than a baby. The mom can report how she feels, communicate with her doctor, and make decisions; a doctor can physically observe and assess her. There are many unknowns when it comes to your baby. Your baby is inside you, so the doctors cannot physically assess them. Many times, the doctors must rely on you to communicate things about your baby, like if your baby is moving or if you are having any pain in your abdomen.

While an ultrasound can essentially "see" your baby, it is limited in what it can detect. It is beneficial and shows you if your baby is head down, how much amniotic fluid surrounds them, and estimates how big your baby is.

Hands down, the best way to determine how your baby is doing is their heart rate. It is the best moment-to-moment information the doctor will have on your baby.

#2 Talk to Me Baby: Fetal Monitoring

When you arrive at the hospital, one of the first things your delivery team will do is start the fetal monitor. This device records your baby's heart rate and displays it next to your bed, along with your contractions. As your baby's heart rate and your contractions are very important during labor, it is also displayed at the nurses' station and the room designated for the doctors. Your private physician should also be able to review the fetal monitor remotely.

My favorite explanation that described the importance of the baby's heart rate during labor occurred during the deposition of an expert witness. The expert explained how a baby talks to the doctor from inside their mom; it is through their heart rate:

> The only way a fetus can speak to a doctor
> is through the fetal heart rate, so you have to

take it very seriously when there are changes.
(*Expert Witness*)

This means a baby can talk to whoever understands their heart rate, including you. If you can interpret the heart rate, you will know if your baby is saying, "Everything is good," or, "Hey, these contractions are coming too close, and I need some more downtime between them. Please turn down the Pitocin." You can know exactly which statement your baby is making when you look at their heart rate.

It is crucial to keep in mind that during contractions, your baby may be trying to communicate to you or your delivery team. It is important to pay close attention to your baby's cues and signals during a contraction. For example, if your baby is struggling during a contraction, their heart rate may drop as the intensity of the contraction increases. Likewise, if your baby's heart rate remains reassuring during a contraction, your baby is likely happy. Chapter 9 provides detailed information on how to interpret your baby's heart rate, allowing you to better understand what your baby is communicating to you and the delivery team during labor.

#3 Baby's Lifeline: Placenta and Umbilical Cord

Your baby depends on two vital things to survive: the placenta and the umbilical cord. Both are located in the uterus with your baby and work together to provide oxygen-rich blood and nutrients that your baby needs to grow and develop.

Foundation of Labor and Delivery

They also play a crucial role by providing the oxygen your baby relies on to survive and get through labor.

The placenta attaches to the wall of the uterus and absorbs the necessary nutrients from the mother's blood to feed the baby. The umbilical cord serves as a lifeline between the placenta and your baby. One end of the cord is attached to your baby's belly button, while the other is attached to the placenta. The cord contains a vein that transfers oxygen and nutrients from the placenta to the baby and two arteries that transfer low-oxygen blood back to the placenta.

The placenta and umbilical cord must remain intact and functioning during labor to avoid any complications for your baby. If the umbilical cord becomes compressed, it can lead to a lack of oxygen-rich blood reaching the baby, which can result in complications. To help explain the seriousness of cord compression, experts often use the analogy of a deep-sea diver relying on a hose for oxygen. If someone were to step on or compress the hose, the diver would be unable to receive the oxygen they need to survive and would have to return to the boat. Similarly, the umbilical cord is like a hose, and it must remain uncompressed to transfer oxygen-rich blood to the baby.

Equally important is the role of the placenta during labor. The placenta is responsible for providing the umbilical cord with the oxygen-rich blood that the baby needs to survive. If the placenta detaches from the wall of the uterus or is not functioning properly, it can also cause problems for the baby. This is because the cord will have a decreased amount or no oxygen-rich blood to transfer to the baby, which can lead to complications during labor.

Fortunately, the fetal monitor can help detect any issues with the placenta or umbilical cord during labor. The monitor can alert you to changes in your baby's heart rate, which may indicate if something is wrong with the umbilical cord or placenta. For example, a gradual decrease in your baby's heart rate during a contraction could suggest an issue with the placenta, while a more abrupt drop could mean a problem with the umbilical cord. Chapter 9 will go over the difference between the two in more detail.

#4 Home of the Baby: The Uterus

The uterus plays a crucial role in pregnancy, as it provides a safe and comfortable home for your growing baby. The baby, placenta, and umbilical cord are all housed within the uterus, with the baby being surrounded by a protective sac filled with amniotic fluid. This fluid acts as a cushion that your baby is floating in. The baby is able to breathe in this fluid and essentially lives underwater until birth.

The "bag of water" holds the amniotic fluid which surrounds the baby in the womb. Sometimes, it can break naturally because of the baby's movements or the pressure from the contractions. A doctor might break it too, but only if the baby's head is in the right position. The baby's head must be down, pushing up against the door out of the uterus called the cervix. If the doctor breaks the water when the baby's head is not in the right position, it can be dangerous for the baby. The umbilical cord may come out with the water and will reduce the amount of oxygen that the baby receives, also called a cord prolapse. If this happens, it is an obstetrical emergency that will likely end with a C-section as the doctor cannot push the umbilical cord back into the uterus.

When the water breaks, it is important to observe the color of the fluid. Clear fluid is normal, but if it is a brownish or greenish color, it could indicate that the baby has had a bowel movement, which is called meconium. If the fluid is anything but clear, it must be reported to your doctor as soon as possible.

The cervix is considered the door of the uterus. It is the baby's way out, unless a C-section is performed where the doctor makes their own door and pulls the baby out. From the door, the baby will go through a tunnel known as the birth canal. This leads to the vaginal opening and the outside world. Getting through the door, or the cervix, is a big part of labor. Your delivery team will be monitoring and assessing your cervix as your labor progresses.

#5 How Far Is Your Baby Out the Door: Vaginal Examinations

During labor, doctors monitor how far baby is out the door and into the birth canal, and how your cervix is changing by performing vaginal examinations. These examinations measure three things:
- Cervical dilation: Measures how big is the door getting for the baby to pass through, which gradually

widens as labor progresses. Dilation starts at 1 cm and is complete at 10 cm.
- Cervical effacement: This refers to how thin and short the cervix becomes as the baby moves down into the birth canal. Effacement starts at 0% and is complete at 100%, indicating that the cervix is ready for delivery.
- Station of the baby: How far down in the birth canal is your baby? This refers to the position of the baby's head in relation to the pelvis. The range of -5 to -1 indicates that the baby's head is not yet engaged in the cervix, while the range of +1 to +5 indicates that the baby's head is descending through the birth canal. The baby's head is at the vaginal opening when it reaches +5.

Medical staff typically perform vaginal exams when you are admitted to labor and delivery. Thereafter, they may be repeated every 2 to 4 hours or as needed. For instance, if you have the urge to push, or if your baby's heart rate becomes concerning.

#6 Pushing Your Baby Out the Door: Contractions

Your baby is not leaving on their own, so your body produces contractions to help your baby through the door or the cervix. This will help open the cervix and clear the path for your baby. A contraction is when the muscles of your uterus tighten up like a fist and then relax. Babies are getting squeezed with every contraction, which decreases the oxygen to your baby as the natural part of labor. This happens in every labor, and babies are made to handle the decreases in oxygen and the stress of the contractions.

If it is time to "boot" your baby out of their comfy home, the doctor may want to give you Pitocin. This will make your body contract and push your baby out the door. Keep in mind that if your baby is not ready to leave home, Pitocin is basically forcing them out by making your uterus contract. The contractions from Pitocin are typically managed differently than the natural ones you have without this medication. If you are contracting more than you should on Pitocin, they may decrease the Pitocin, stop the Pitocin, or even give you another drug to slow down the contractions. However, if these same contractions are natural and your baby is doing okay, the delivery team will likely not intervene unless needed.

#7 Fetal Reserve: How Many Contractions Can Your Baby Handle?

Labor is hard on both the mom and the baby. It is not just the mother who is putting in the work while the baby is comfortably relaxing in their last few moments in paradise. The most difficult aspect of labor for both the mother and her baby is the relentless contractions, especially during a longer labor. While mothers have the option of receiving an epidural for some relief, babies do not have that same luxury.

To better understand what babies go through during contractions, one doctor shared an analogy. Imagine going underwater and holding your breath. When you resurface, you gasp for air. This is comparable to what a baby experiences during each contraction—they are holding their breath underwater. Now imagine doing this for a long time, with contractions becoming stronger and more frequent. This should help you understand why your baby may get tired or stressed during a longer labor.

In legal cases involving babies, doctors often refer to a concept known as "fetal reserve." This refers to the baby's ability to handle stress during labor and delivery. The baby's reserves help them recover from contractions and any other stressors that may reduce their oxygen supply during labor. However, these reserves are not unlimited, and with each contraction, they gradually decrease. While there is no way to measure your baby's reserves during labor, you can tell that the reserves may be depleting when there are concerning changes in your baby's heart rate (*see Chapter 9*). The goal of your delivery team is to pick up on these changes and deliver your baby before the reserves are depleted.

The concept of "fetal reserves" has gained significance in the legal world. This concept is often explained to juries during trials and discussed during expert depositions to illustrate the fact that a baby can only handle so much stress during labor before getting into trouble. It is important to note that not all medical professionals are familiar with or use this concept, as it may be employed more frequently in a legal context than during actual labor and deliveries.

#8 When Is Your Baby Coming Out? Stages of Labor

Getting your baby out the door may take some time. The medical community created stages of labor and phases of labor so they can better understand how your labor is progressing and when the baby may arrive. Here is a more detailed breakdown of each stage:

- The first stage of labor is the longest and is divided into two phases: the latent phase and the active phase. During the latent phase, the cervix dilates slowly, and contractions are more spaced out. This phase ends once the cervix is dilated to 6 cm, and the active phase begins. The active phase is when contractions become more intense and frequent, and moms typically dilate more rapidly from 6 cm to 10 cm.

- The second stage of labor is the pushing stage, which is the most intense stage for both the mom and the baby. The length of this stage can vary, lasting from a few minutes to a few hours.

- The third stage of labor occurs after the baby is born and the placenta is delivered. The uterus continues to contract after delivery, causing the placenta to detach from the uterine wall. This can happen naturally or with the help of doctors, depending on the situation. The purpose of medical assistance is to avoid severe blood loss following birth.

Being aware of the stage of labor you are in can be crucial, as it can form the basis of the recommendations made by your delivery team.

#9 Delivery Room or Operating Room

You will deliver your baby in one of two spots at the hospital, either in your delivery room or in the operating room. You will be in the operating room if you need a C-section or, in some cases, a vaginal delivery that may have to convert quickly to a C-section. If you need an operative vaginal delivery, you may end up in the operating room. This is a sterile room where they perform the surgical procedures. Otherwise, an uncomplicated vaginal birth should be in your labor and delivery room. After your baby arrives, if the hospital has a postpartum unit, you will be transferred to that area where you can recover and hang out with your baby.

#10 After Birth Care: Neonatal Care

Neonatal care is the care your baby receives after they are born. When a legal case comes in, the first two things we look at are the baby's APGAR scores and cord blood gases. Doctors use the APGAR score to evaluate your baby's health at 1 and 5 minutes, and sometimes 10 minutes after birth. They assess your baby's skin color, pulse, reflexes, muscle tone, and respiratory effort and give your baby 0 to 2 points for each category. Anything above 7 is considered normal, 4 to 6 is low, and for 3 and under, your baby needs medical attention. Scores of 10 are uncommon, as most babies typically score 1 point for color.

The other important piece of information is the baby's cord blood gases. After birth, they take blood samples from the umbilical cord and send them to the lab, which calculates your baby's gases at birth. The two blood gases from the umbilical cord are the venous and the arterial. Your baby's arterial blood gas sample will tell you how oxygenated your baby is at birth. The venous cord blood gas tells you how the placenta is functioning. This is a more oxygenated blood sample, so the venous blood gases are typically higher than the arterial blood gases.

It is good to know cord blood gases exist and is a measurement of how well oxygenated your baby is at birth. A normal range for an arterial cord blood gas is pH of 7.25, and a normal range venous cord blood gas has a pH of 7.33.

Chapter 3

The Dream Team: The Role of Your Delivery Team

Whether you are arriving at the hospital because you are having contractions, your water broke, or you are going in for induction of labor, it is time. As part of being ready for the big day, you must have a good understanding of your delivery team. In a legal baby case, the delivery team is known as the fact witnesses. These fact witnesses are the most crucial part of the case. It is their care that is at issue and what they did or did not do that will be the center of the case. Similar to the legal world, your delivery team is the most important part of your labor and delivery. They will help guide you and bring your baby into this world.

In legal cases, I do not get to pick the delivery team that would make up the fact witnesses for the defense. These are the fact witnesses, no matter if I like them or not. There is no swapping out fact witnesses in a legal case. While attorneys can stack the legal team with the best people to win a case, they cannot select the best fact witnesses. Most of the time, the fact witnesses in a case are the team of people scheduled to work that day or night. Likewise, your delivery team will consist of people who are scheduled to work. Babies come when they are ready. There could be a six-week window when the baby could arrive. Having a stacked delivery team for the day your baby says, "It is time," is almost impossible. There is no way to know when your baby will arrive, unless you have a scheduled C-section.

When it is time to meet the fact witnesses on a delivery team, one of the most important things I do as an attorney is form my initial impression of the delivery team. I closely listen to each witness I meet with and watch them as I determine whether they will be a good or bad witness in front of a jury. Are they credible, truthful, kind, and smart? How do they explain things, and does it make sense? Are they experienced or inexperienced? What is my instinct telling me? As we meet, the attorney analysis goes into full swing.

As you meet your delivery team for the first time, you need to do a similar analysis. Instead of thinking, "How will the delivery team appear in front of a jury?" you need to make your initial impression on how they will care for you during labor and delivery. You need to engage your brain and heart as you ask yourself if you trust them. Do you like them? Are they giving you all of your options? Are they truthful? What are your instincts telling you?

The Dream Team

When I am evaluating a delivery team as fact witnesses, I categorize them. If I am overly impressed with a delivery team,

I describe them as the "dream team." This team gives good care and will be liked by a jury. The people on this team are good communicators, smart, kind, and trying to do what is best for the mom and her baby. This is the team that you want delivering your baby. You may be thinking, how can a delivery team be a dream team when something went wrong during labor and delivery? This is because not all cases involve someone doing something wrong. Things happen during labor and delivery beyond the control of humans. This book is about learning from the other cases, the preventable ones where mistakes were made.

Team with a Bad Apple

The next category is a step below the dream team. If there is someone on the delivery team that is not a good witness or person, but the rest of the team are excellent witnesses, I categorize them as the team with the bad apple. While the "ostrich with its head in the sand" approach sounds appealing, this is an issue that must be confronted early on, given how important the fact witnesses are in a case. To the same degree, if you have a bad apple on your delivery team, this issue needs to be addressed early on.

How to handle a bad apple should have been covered with your doctor during your pregnancy, as every hospital and doctors' office is different. If you are sitting on labor and delivery with someone you are not a fan of on your team, there are a couple of things you can do. First, get a hold of your doctor and let them know you have concerns about someone on the team. If you are deep into labor, someone else should be making this call. This is a good time to have your baby advocate step in and help you.

When you speak to your doctor, they should do one of two things: either give you a good solution or come to the hospital. Keep in mind that the doctor who is on-call or going to deliver your baby has positioned themselves to be able to drop everything and come to the hospital to deliver your baby. For this reason, they have the ability to come see you anytime and help you with your concerns about someone on your delivery team.

In the unlikely event that your doctor brushes you off and does nothing, there are other nurses and doctors at the hospital that you can talk to. This could be someone else on your delivery team or another doctor or nurse on the floor. The goal is to replace the person you are concerned about with someone else, so you feel comfortable during labor and delivery.

In one legal baby case, there were two nurses. The first nurse was fresh out of training and quickly realized that she disliked labor and delivery. She was miserable, and, in less than a year, she left her job. The second nurse was born to be a labor and delivery nurse. She had 20 years of experience and loved her job. Her mission in life was to be the best nurse possible and help moms bring their babies safely into this world. That particular evening on labor and delivery, it was the luck of the draw on which patient got which nurse. One lucky patient got the good nurse, and one unlucky patient got the inexperienced nurse who did not like her job. It should not be hard to figure out which nurse's patient sued the hospital for bad care.

In this case example, the inexperienced nurse was literally a self-proclaimed very bad labor and delivery nurse, which is why she left the field so fast after starting. If you get a nurse like this and you raise a concern with your doctor or another nurse, they probably are already on the same page as you. Once you speak up, it will get the ball rolling toward a solution. Remember, the experienced nurse cannot stick her head in your room and warn you about your nurse, but once you say something, they can step in and do what they do best—help you.

Bush League

The last category is "bush league." This is when two or more people on the delivery team are not good witnesses. This could be the blind leading the blind or a complete disregard for what is best for the mom and her baby. When these are the fact witnesses, early settlement with no chance of trial is recommended. It is very unlikely that this will be your delivery team. These teams are rare and were more prominent in the early 2000s at the beginning of my career. Back then, legal baby cases were more prevalent, but after the hospitals hemorrhaged money for years, there was a corresponding improvement in the delivery teams.

If you find yourself in labor and delivery feeling uneasy about more than one person on your delivery team, your private doctor may be part of the problem. If this proves true, reaching out to them directly may not be an option. However, there are other avenues you can explore. For instance, contact a different doctor in the same practice to express your concerns. It is possible that the doctor taking charge of the deliveries that day may not align with your views, causing you to feel uncertain. By speaking with another doctor in the practice, you may be able to find a solution.

A different avenue is finding a nurse on labor and delivery that you can trust. You can always ask to speak to the charge nurse, who is the nurse in charge of supervising the other nurses. Nurses serve as patient advocates and can assist you with your concerns and any problems you may be having with your delivery team, even if they are not directly responsible for your care.

If those options do not work, you could try to find a different doctor at the hospital who can assist you. If an "in-house" doctor is available, they may be able to take over your care, depending on the circumstances. However, this may not always be possible, as different hospitals have different rules.

Switching hospitals may be another option, but it comes with its own set of risks. It is something you should only consider as a last resort, depending on the distance to the other hospital and the state of your labor. Ultimately, while it is crucial to prioritize the safety and well-being of both you and your little one, you need to weigh the risks of switching hospitals versus staying at the hospital with a delivery team that you are uneasy about.

Here is the deal. It is extremely unlikely that you will have this type of delivery team if you prepare for the big day. Reading this book alone, you will have already covered everything with your doctor and researched your hospital to avoid even the potential of this type of team. As I have seen these teams on occasion, my goal was to provide you with guidance on the off chance that this was your team.

Private Physician

The doctor or doctors you have been seeing during your pregnancy are considered your private physician(s). This is likely the only person you get to select for your delivery team, which is good because this is the person who is ultimately in charge of your labor. You are their patient, which means the delivery team at the hospital must contact your doctor for all decisions and keep them updated on your labor. Since your private doctor is in charge, they must approve the plan for your labor. You may be thinking, "Why is my doctor not at the hospital during my labor if they are in charge?"

It is true; the person ultimately responsible for your labor is usually not at the hospital during the process itself. Your private doctor will be contacted once you are admitted to labor and delivery. Your doctor may come in and check on you at the hospital. Otherwise, you may not see them until delivery. The one exception is if your doctor takes call or works a shift at the hospital when you are in labor. Then, you may have the luxury of having your private doctor at the hospital for part or all of your labor.

Your private doctor plays an important role in your labor and delivery. There is a lot to consider when choosing a good doctor, which is why an entire chapter is dedicated to picking "The Good Doctor" (*see Chapter 4*).

Nurses

Your nurse will play a huge role in your labor and delivery. They are the eyes and the ears of your doctor. You will see your nurse more than anyone else on your delivery team. They have a big job. If there is an issue with the baby's heart rate or any other concern during labor, they are responsible for notifying the doctor. If this is an induction of labor, the nurse is responsible for increasing or decreasing Pitocin. The nurse is the main person writing in your medical chart. Nurses are the designated advocates for you and your baby. As your advocate, they are responsible for making sure that all recommendations and decisions are in the best interest of you and your baby.

If a nurse has a concern about you or your baby during labor, your nurse may either contact your doctor, resident, or midwife. Depending on the hospital, nurses do not always contact your doctor directly. Sometimes they alert the resident or a midwife, and they will come check on you and the baby first before your doctor is contacted. Hospitals and doctors' offices vary on the line of communication back to your doctor, so it is important to determine who is updating your doctor about your labor.

Labor and delivery nurses are a special breed of people. They dedicate themselves to helping moms bring new life into the world. They must work with all types of doctors from different offices and interact with the public on a regular basis. They have long hours and are immune to blood, vomit, and bowel movements. They do things that most of us cannot imagine. In legal baby cases, nurses show more human emotion than any other person on the delivery team. This may be because they are connected to their patients in a way that cannot be explained. You not only want to be nice to your nurse because they are the first line of communication to your doctor, but because it takes a special person to do what they do.

Residents

Most large hospitals have a residency program, and we refer to these hospitals as teaching institutions. This is where students studying to become doctors get their hands-on experience. After completing college studies and finishing medical school, they start their residency. They have gone through years of studying and are now ready to practice medicine on moms in labor. They are learning the ropes and are inexperienced. This is where they learn how to do ultrasounds, and perform vaginal examinations and C-sections.

If there is a concern about your baby during labor, at teaching institutions, the nurse will contact the resident first, in most cases, to come to your room and assess you. The resident will then be responsible for contacting your private doctor to give them updates about their assessment. If something is very concerning, the resident may also involve the in-house doctor at the hospital. Residents have a crucial job, as they are responsible for updating your doctor on your labor progress and how your baby is doing during labor.

Over the years, numerous stories about residents have highlighted their tendency to drive nurses up the wall. While it is important to note that this is not universal among all residents, some can become a little arrogant toward nurses as they start acting like doctors and learning the ropes. This can particularly upset senior nurses, especially when there is a disagreement between the two parties.

If you find yourself in a situation where a nurse disagrees with a resident, involving your private doctor or the hospital doctor may be a wise move. However, it is not always immediately apparent when there is a conflict between the two, and you may need to read between the lines. For example, if your nurse tells you one thing and the resident comes in with an opposing opinion shortly after, it could indicate a behind-the-scenes disagreement. In such situations, it may be helpful to take your nurse's opinion into consideration, especially if they have a wealth of experience and you trust them.

Midwife

You may have a midwife involved in the delivery of your baby. You can choose to have a midwife (seeing one prenatally), or the hospital may assign a midwife to you in labor and delivery. Doctors' offices also employ midwives, so you may be seeing one depending on the office.

A midwife can manage your labor and deliver your baby. They cannot perform C-sections or use a vacuum or forceps, but they usually have quick access to a doctor when needed. Midwives pride themselves on providing patients with emotional support and comfort during their labor and delivery. If a midwife oversees your labor, you will likely see them more than you would a doctor. Many will also give air support to the nurses to help them with their patients, particularly if the nurse gets busy with another patient on the labor and delivery unit.

On-Call or In-House Doctor at the Hospital

Most hospitals have a doctor available 24/7 to assist patients in labor. This doctor, also known as the "in-house" or "on-call" doctor, typically works 12-hour shifts to provide support to patients or assist private physicians who are not present at the hospital. If an emergency arises and your private doctor is unavailable, the in-house doctor can step in to provide necessary medical attention promptly. At teaching institutions, the in-house doctor may also supervise residents.

While the in-house doctor may not be your primary physician, they can assume responsibility for your care if you do not have a prenatal doctor or if you are out of town when you go into labor.

Although your private doctor is ultimately responsible for your care, the in-house doctor plays a crucial role if there are any concerns regarding your baby's health or if your private doctor is unable to reach the hospital before you give birth. In these cases, the in-house doctor can provide quick intervention, which is especially important if your private doctor is not near the hospital.

Anesthesiologist

If you need an epidural or C-section, an anesthesiologist or CRNA (certified registered nurse anesthetist) will become part of your delivery team. They will place your epidural, which will give you relief from painful contractions. They are also in charge of making sure you do not feel pain during a C-section. An epidural numbs you from your belly button to your upper legs by injecting an anesthetic into the epidural space of your spine.

Pediatrician or Neonatologist

In the event that something happens prior to delivery, such as a rush to the operating room or concerns about the baby, a specialized medical professional will be present during delivery. A pediatrician, hospitalist, or neonatologist will be on-hand (at most hospitals) to closely monitor the baby's health and ensure that they are adapting well to their new environment. These medical professionals specialize in newborn care and are equipped to provide any necessary assistance to help the baby make a smooth transition into the outside world.

Triage

Upon arrival at the hospital, you may go to triage first. If you go to the hospital for contractions or your water broke, this is the area where you will initially be evaluated. The person who performs the evaluation can be a resident, physician assistant, or nurse. The first step is starting the fetal monitor so that they can see the baby's heart rate. They go through your medical history, why you came to the hospital, and ask questions about your pregnancy and baby.

Following the initial assessment, the person who evaluated you will contact your private doctor to discuss their findings. Together, they make a plan. If you are in labor or need to be admitted to labor and delivery for any reason, you will be transferred to that area of the hospital. If you are not in labor or there is no reason for you to be at the hospital, they may send you home.

Pro Tip

In legal baby cases, the care and time spent in triage can be very important. If mom is going to be admitted to labor and delivery, she will wait in triage while they get her room ready. If the hospital is busy or it is the night shift, there could be a longer waiting period. The triage area is not heavily staffed and new patients may be coming in who need the medical staff's attention. In some cases, a mom is left in limbo. The decision has been made to move her out of triage, but she must wait before being transferred to labor and delivery. It is during this time when not a lot of attention is being paid to mom that something can and has gone wrong.

If you get stuck in limbo, it will be important for you or your baby advocate to have the staff in triage regularly check on you and your baby. It is also important to make sure the baby's heart rate continues to graph next to your bed. In legal baby cases, moms have been in triage for hours without monitoring the baby's heart rate, which has become a big issue in cases. As best you can, try to shorten the amount of time you are in triage if the plan is to move you to labor and delivery.

Labor and Delivery Unit

Upon arrival at the labor and delivery department, the first thing the nurse will do is connect you to the fetal monitor. You may be asked some of the same questions as during the triage process, and your vitals and blood pressure will be checked. Blood and urine samples may also be taken, and a vaginal examination will be performed to assess your cervix. Depending on your individual circumstances, an ultrasound may be performed to estimate fetal weight, check the level of amniotic fluid, or check the baby's position.

Once you are settled in, the delivery team will discuss different options or recommendations with you. For example, if your baby is breech, they may offer an external cephalic version to rotate the baby into a head-down position, or a C-section may be recommended. If you are experiencing strong contractions and pain, an epidural may be offered; if your labor needs to be jumpstarted, Pitocin may be recommended. It is important to be prepared to make decisions when you arrive to the labor and delivery unit.

When you are admitted to labor and delivery, you will meet your delivery team, starting with the nurse. Depending on the hospital or your personal preferences, you may also meet residents, midwives, or anesthesiologists. The in-house doctor may also visit you. If your doctor is available, they may come see you as well. This is your opportunity to get to know your team and ensure you feel comfortable and confident in their care.

Pro Tip

In legal baby cases, the triage assessment versus the labor and delivery assessment often has conflicting information. This is likely because two different people are taking your history and doing your initial assessment. For instance, in a couple of cases, the triage person charted a decrease in the baby's movement since the day before, but the initial assessment in labor and delivery said that the baby had been moving normally. Make sure you are clearly communicating with each person who is writing in your chart. A decrease in fetal movement for a day can be significant and will probably influence the delivery team's recommendations for your labor.

Two Different Shifts on Labor and Delivery

Delivery team shifts are 12 hours long, in the range of 7:00 to 7:00. Some teams start at 6:00 and end at 6:00. After 12 hours, the delivery team gets off work, and a new delivery team will start their shift. The new team will get a report from the team getting off work. The old team gives an oral update on the progress of your labor and anything else the oncoming team should know about you as a patient. The oncoming team can look at the fetal monitor or your medical records to find out any further information about your labor.

There are two shifts, the day and the night shift. In most hospitals, the day shift has everyone working, so the labor and delivery unit operates at its maximum potential. The night shift at many hospitals runs lean. Not as many people work at night, including residents and doctors. The hospital may not have all the operating rooms up and running. In many smaller hospitals, at night, the anesthesiologist and the pediatrician go home and are on-call, which means they may be up to 20 or 30 minutes away from the hospital.

The Distracted Delivery Team

You arrive at the hospital in labor; you have read this book three times and are ready to meet your delivery team. You are excited to form your initial impression of your delivery team to determine if you hit the lotto with your dream team. The people on your team come in to meet you, and while you like them, they seem off. Something is up. You are excited and a little nervous, but ready. The team does not seem to have the same enthusiasm.

Since developing your first impression of your team is important, this part of the chapter is equally significant. This is not a free pass for the delivery team, but it will help you understand what you may be walking into. The delivery team brings new life into the world; as we have seen, sometimes there is not a good ending. If you arrive at the hospital in labor after one of these not-good endings to another delivery, you may encounter a team replaying events in their head, conducting internal meetings, or otherwise preoccupied with what just occurred.

While your delivery team may not be "happy-go-lucky" when you arrive, there are some things to consider. Your delivery team was just reminded that we are not immortal, and they will likely be very cautious with your labor. An upset delivery team is what you would expect from a caring and good team. If there is a tragedy on the floor and someone on your delivery team is not fazed, that is who you may want to be concerned about. While they will stay professional and not cry on your shoulder, they may not be telling you a funny story or have the same enthusiasm they displayed earlier in the shift.

Effectively Communicating with Your Delivery Team

Several lessons can be learned from the legal baby cases on why it is important to have good communication with your delivery team. Firstly, it is crucial to understand that a busy labor and delivery unit can lead to communication breakdowns between the team and the mother, potentially resulting in missed details and mistakes. Therefore, it is important to maintain continued communication with your team, particularly if it is a busy day at the hospital.

Secondly, reporting any changes in how you are feeling is critical to ensure prompt attention and appropriate care. In one legal baby case, a mother testified that she experienced severe and constant pain in her abdomen during a Pitocin induction, but did not inform her nurse for several hours. This was surprising, but honest, testimony in the case as mom admitted that she did not tell the nurse. A good rule of thumb is that if you are experiencing anything that a nurse or doctor cannot determine by physically assessing you or looking at you, let them know immediately.

Thirdly, it is important to acknowledge that even good doctors can have bad days, and mistakes can occur if they are not paying attention. Consistent communication and active engagement with your team can help keep them closely attuned to your needs and the progress of your labor.

Finally, keep in mind that basic communication skills apply in labor and delivery. One key to communicating with your team is building a good rapport with them by being kind and nice. Being mean, arrogant, or rude can shut down communication and make your team unengaged. As humans, we tend to be drawn to people who are kind and want to help them, while we tend to avoid those who are rude. This applies to your delivery team as well. By being appreciative and grateful for their hard work, you can get a better response. They may spend more time with you, explain things in more detail, and be more engaging. On the other hand, being rude to your team will only make them want to end the conversation as quickly as possible.

It is essential to remember that emotions can run high during labor and delivery, and people can get easily triggered. If this happens, remember that staying calm and collected will help you and your baby advocate communicate more effectively with the team. Ultimately, your baby's safety is paramount, and your delivery team is responsible for ensuring a safe delivery. Therefore, staying calm and engaging with your team is crucial to help them do their job effectively.

Chapter 4

How to Choose "The Good Doctor"

This chapter explores the world of doctors, covering both the good and the bad, and everything in between. In this chapter, I will share my insights on doctors based on my extensive experience working with them for over 20 years in various professional capacities. Whether I was their attorney because something went wrong during childbirth, or I retained them as an expert witness to hash out a legal baby case, or whether I had to cross-examine a physician on the other side of the case, I have spent a considerable amount of time with doctors. While some interactions have been intense, most physicians who deliver babies are respectful, nice, and professional. In my experience, I have encountered many more great doctors in this field than bad ones. For this chapter, I have used the past 20 years of these interactions with doctors to give you insights to think about, which will help you pick a good doctor.

The Doctor Analysis

I have spent countless hours with doctors analyzing not only labor and delivery, but also the doctor themselves. After each meeting or deposition, I would write a detailed analysis of the doctor's opinions and whether I believed they were a good doctor. I would consider factors such as likability, whether they were articulate, intelligent, credible, and how a jury may perceive them if the case went to trial. However, what I have come to realize is that there is no magic formula that makes a doctor great. Just like us, doctors are humans and have unique personalities and qualities that make them excel at their job.

When it comes to labor and delivery, your doctor plays a pivotal role in guiding you through the process, making important recommendations, and helping you make decisions along the way. To ensure you choose the best possible candidate for the job, it is important to conduct a "doctor analysis." There are many things to take into consideration, many of which are covered later in this chapter. However, when I analyze a doctor, I always fall back on two essential elements: instincts and communication.

#1 Follow Your Instincts

When it comes to selecting a doctor to deliver your baby, trusting your instincts is crucial. While a doctor's credentials and reputation are undoubtedly important, relying solely on these factors is not enough. Further, this process can also be clouded by various factors, including recommendations from family and friends or internet research. While all of these are important to consider, engaging your instincts to help guide you in the decision-making process is essential.

During your first visit, take note of how you feel around the doctor. Do you feel comfortable and relaxed, or are you anxious and on edge? A good doctor should make you feel at ease and should be approachable. If you find yourself feeling nervous or uncomfortable, it could be a sign that they are not the right doctor for you.

You should feel comfortable asking questions and sharing your concerns without feeling judged or embarrassed. If you are holding back or watching what you say, it may be a sign that the doctor is not a good fit for you. As you interact with your doctor, it is not only important to engage your instincts, but to trust them.

It is not uncommon for people to ignore their instincts and end up regretting this later. In fact, I have received many calls from upset parents who did not like their doctor from the start. They did not follow their instincts and look where it got them: on the phone with me. You have instincts for a reason, so do not let them go to waste, or it could land you in a bad spot.

#2 Are They Good Communicators and Listen to You?

Doctors, as witnesses in a legal case, are unique. Some doctors listen carefully to instructions, ask questions, and provide clear and concise answers to questions. They have good eye contact, nod their head when appropriate, and you know they are engaged in the process. These doctors are likable and typically have great communication skills.

On the other hand, some doctors may have difficulties serving as a witness in a legal case due to their poor communication skills. They may struggle to actively listen and may have preconceived notions on how to handle the situation, so they disregard advice from their legal team. As a result, this can hinder their effectiveness as a witness and complicate the legal proceedings.

Similar to a legal case, your doctor's communication skills play a crucial role in the care you will receive, so it is important to consider the doctor's communication style. Do they listen attentively and explain things clearly, or do they seem rushed and dismissive? A good doctor should be willing to take the time to listen to you and address your concerns. They should be transparent and willing to explain their thought process and recommendations.

Good communication means that your doctor can explain medical concepts in plain language, making it easier for you to understand the risks, benefits, and alternatives of your options during labor and delivery. With effective communication, your doctor can help you make informed decisions and ultimately make good choices.

Whether your doctor effectively communicates with the delivery team is equally important as well. Keep in mind that the way your doctor communicates with you may be indicative of how they communicate with the delivery team, who will be providing direct care to you and your baby. The delivery team may also provide recommendations to your doctor based on their initial assessment of you and your baby, and your doctor will work with them to create a plan for your labor and delivery. When your doctor communicates effectively with the delivery team and listens to their recommendations and concerns, it ensures that you receive the best possible care during this crucial time.

The Yoda Imposter

I was in a meeting with a fact witness, and they referred to a doctor as "Yoda." I responded, "Are you calling him Yoda because he looks like Yoda?" I did not think he resembled Yoda, but there was no way we were talking about the same doctor. The witness clarified that we were in fact talking about the same doctor. The witness explained that this doctor was a very wise physician whom no one ever sees. They just hear about the great things he does for his patients. The witness had left this hospital years earlier, so she did not know the scoop on the doctor she called Yoda. I told her to do an internet search with his legal name as he was being accused of doing some bad things to his patients.

The question of how a bad doctor gets the nickname "Yoda" is intriguing. However, the purpose of this book is not to explore that matter, but rather to learn from it. This lesson teaches us that a doctor's good reputation does not necessarily equate to good care.

A good reputation is highly valued in the medical field, as doctors rely on the approval of their colleagues and patients to secure more work and referrals. Unfortunately, some doctors can maintain a good reputation despite not providing good care, as was the case with the doctor referred to as "Yoda."

The doctor was able to fool those around him, with his good reputation likely playing a role in that. However, at some point, patients' instincts and intuition began to question his actions, leading to his eventual exposure.

If you feel uncomfortable with a doctor, despite everyone else praising them, follow your instincts and intuition. You are likely correct. Just because everyone else likes the doctor and may refer to them as "Yoda," this may be far from true. At a minimum, seek a second opinion from a doctor who is not affiliated with the physician you may be questioning. This applies to every doctor you encounter in life, not just the one delivering your baby. Remember that a good reputation does not always equate to good care.

Doctor's CV or Résumé

In the legal world, a doctor's curriculum vitae, or CV, is a document that helps build their credibility as an expert witness. At the start of their deposition, attorneys will often go over the doctor's CV with them to ask various questions about their training and background. When it comes time for trial, the CV of each doctor who testifies is presented to the jury so they can review their credentials while they deliberate.

A doctor's CV is a comprehensive list of everything they have accomplished professionally. However, the length of a doctor's CV does not necessarily reflect their competence or expertise. For doctors who are in the trenches every day, caring for patients and delivering babies, their CV may be shorter. But for doctors who have pursued research interests, given lectures, and received numerous awards, their CV may be longer.

Although it is not typical for doctors to offer their CVs to patients, it is essential to be aware of their existence. If you desire to learn more about your physician's qualifications and experience, you can request a copy of their CV. Alternatively, you could visit their website, but keep in mind that it may only feature a professional biography. Their CV is formatted like a résumé and includes more detailed information about education, training, work history, publications, and other relevant accomplishments.

Look Up Your Doctor

When searching for a doctor, it is important to do your research. Doctors are licensed professionals, which means you can look them up and see if they have any dings on their medical license in your state. If you know they are licensed in other states, look them up in those states as well.

Additionally, you can search for their name on your local court's website to see if they have any prior or current lawsuits. If they have been named as a defendant in a few lawsuits, this may be a red flag, especially if the doctor has not been practicing that long. However, if you decide to pay a small fee to view the complaint filed against the doctor, keep in mind that the allegations may not accurately reflect the doctor. In some cases, attorneys are required to include all possible allegations in the complaint, even if they are unsure about the accuracy of the allegation. If you are currently receiving treatment from a doctor with prior lawsuits and have any concerns, it may be worth asking them about the cases and what happened.

Labor and Delivery Nurses Know Things

Labor and delivery nurses are a treasure trove of information. They have an incredible ability to store vast amounts of data about doctors in their memory banks. As soon as they hear or see something about a doctor, they make a mental note and file it away for future reference. It is fascinating how easily they can recall this information, even when it is buried deep in their subconscious, simply by hearing the doctor's name.

If you have access to a labor and delivery nurse, it is worth asking them for advice on local doctors. If they do not have any personal experience with the doctor in question, they may be able to put you in touch with a nursing colleague who does. Depending on their level of familiarity and trust with you, nurses may be willing to share their knowledge of local doctors. Those who have worked in a hospital for an extended period have an impressive wealth of information and can provide valuable insights into which doctors are the best.

However, it is not advisable to approach nurses you do not know and ask for their opinions about doctors out of the blue. A better approach is to utilize your social network to find a connection to a local labor and delivery nurse. With a little creativity, you are sure to find someone who can help you navigate the local labor and delivery scene.

Different Doctors: Different Styles

While writing this book, I had an intriguing conversation with a labor and delivery nurse about two doctors with opposing approaches: Dr. Jones and Dr. Smith. The nurse had complaints about both doctors, but for entirely different reasons.

Dr. Smith was highly involved in her patients' labor and would constantly call the nurses' station to ensure that they were taking specific actions for her patient. She had the capability to remotely review the baby's heart rate and she would monitor it closely, even when not at the hospital. The nurse found her continuous calls to the nurses' station annoying, especially because she had already completed most of the tasks before the doctor called.

On the other hand, Dr. Jones was the complete opposite. He did not review the baby's heart rate unless requested by a nurse and did not actively monitor his patients during labor. He relied solely on the nurses to contact him if there was a problem or if it was time for delivery. Unfortunately, the nurses did not like to call him unless it was urgent because he would often leave labor and delivery and would tell them not to call him unless it was necessary, particularly if it was late evening.

Dr. Smith and Dr. Jones have completely different management styles. Dr. Smith is highly involved and proactive, while Dr. Jones is more hands-off and reactive. When choosing a doctor, it is essential to consider the pros and cons of each management style.

Dr. Smith's involvement can be comforting and reassuring for some patients who want to be closely monitored throughout their labor. However, her constant calls and interventions may feel overwhelming and invasive for others.

On the other hand, Dr. Jones' more relaxed approach may be preferred by patients who value autonomy and want to be in control of their own labor. However, his lack of involvement may be concerning for patients who desire more medical attention and supervision.

Ultimately, when searching for a doctor, it is important to find one whose management style aligns with your personal preferences and values.

Generic Care versus Patient-Specific Care

Childbirth is a unique and individual experience for every patient. No two people are the same; therefore, no two deliveries are the same. Patients are all different, from their history, prenatal course, body, symptoms, etc. When a doctor guides a patient through childbirth, there is no set formula to follow. The doctor must rely on their education, training, and experience combined with a patient's history, prenatal course, symptoms, and other factors. It is a balance of everything they have learned and know versus you as an individual.

The balance of the two is called patient-specific care. It is this type of care that you want during childbirth.

On the other hand, cookie-cutter care is a generic approach that is applied to most patients without taking into account their individual circumstances. This is the care and recommendations that are virtually the same for most moms. This type of care can be seen when a doctor induces labor or breaks a patient's water at a certain time just because it is convenient for them. It is important to ensure that any recommendations made by your doctor are in the best interest of you and your baby and not simply a routine procedure.

Your health is unique, and it is important that your care is too. Do not be afraid to speak up and ask your doctor about their recommendations. Understanding the reasoning behind their decisions will help you make informed choices that are specific to your needs. For example, if your doctor suggests breaking your water at 7:00 a.m., ask if it is because they are trying to speed up your labor for a specific reason, or if it is just a routine procedure so they can be home for dinner. Asking these questions can help you receive patient-specific care, which will enable you to make better decisions during childbirth.

Battle of Doctors: Different Opinions

In every legal case involving the delivery of a baby, attorneys representing both the family and the hospital will retain expert witnesses—doctors who review the medical records of the mother and her baby. These doctors give their opinions about whether the care provided during labor and delivery was good care or bad care. The lawyers then decide whether to use these opinions in their case or to look for another doctor with a different opinion. This is easy to do because different doctors have different opinions.

The opinions of the expert witnesses are a big part of the case, as these doctors opine on what should or should not have been done during a mom's labor and delivery. The legal baby world exists because doctors on opposite sides of the case have different opinions, meaning the doctors retained by the family in a case will have completely different views than those retained by the hospital. Ultimately, these cases come down to a battle of the doctors, and in some cases, a jury must decide which doctor's opinion is more credible.

It is not just on the opposing sides of a case where doctors disagree. I have had many cases where two well-known doctors from the same hospital give me completely opposite opinions about the exact same care and management of a mother in labor. Just to be clear, these doctors were on the same side of the case and personally retained by me to review the mom's and baby's medical records. One doctor told me everything was done perfectly, and the other was very critical of the same care.

Doctors' opinions in legal baby cases can differ in nearly every aspect of labor and delivery. For example, some doctors may criticize the decision to artificially rupture the mother's bag of water, while others may not see it as a cause for concern. During an induction, one group of doctors may believe

How to Choose "The Good Doctor"

that the contractions are too frequent, while another may not view them as problematic. Some doctors may fault a nurse for failing to notify a physician when the baby's heart rate becomes worrisome, while others may not consider it necessary. With regard to C-sections, some doctors may feel that it took too long to decide to perform the surgery, while others may believe that the procedure was timely.

The fact that doctors may differ in their definitions of quality care means that your doctor's approach to managing your labor and delivery may vary from that of another physician in your community. For instance, in monitoring the baby's heart rate, one doctor may suggest using an internal monitor, while another may be satisfied with an external one. Similarly, when administering Pitocin, one doctor may increase the dose slowly, whereas another may administer it more frequently and at higher doses. It is important to understand that medical recommendations can vary significantly between doctors, and it is not uncommon for one physician to disagree with another's approach.

Fortunately, even though doctors may have varying opinions, the good news is that you should be able to find one who aligns with your preferences and beliefs regarding labor and delivery. When I looked for a doctor, I made it a point to look for one who followed a low-risk approach and was overly cautious. However, your approach to this may differ, and you may prefer a doctor who takes a more hands-off approach. Once you have figured out what kind of doctor you want to deliver your baby, you should be able to find one or more doctors who share your perspective and values.

A Doctor's Privileges

When it comes to delivering babies, understanding your doctor's privileges is important. A doctor's privileges determine the hospitals where they can deliver babies. In order to be approved to deliver babies at a particular hospital, a doctor must meet the hospital's criteria, including having the necessary training, experience, and qualifications.

Without these privileges, your doctor cannot deliver your baby at a particular hospital. It is important to understand that even if your doctor has privileges at one hospital, they may not have them at another. Therefore, when choosing a doctor to deliver your baby, it is essential to consider their hospital privileges and ensure they align with your preferred hospital.

Finding the Right Doctor for You

When searching for the right doctor to deliver your baby, asking questions is important. While doing your own research is valuable, meeting with your doctor and gathering key information that will affect your labor and delivery is crucial. Even though you may not be thinking too much about labor and delivery during your initial meeting, it is important to find out this information to make an informed decision about your doctor.

Getting to know your doctor early on in your pregnancy is a good idea, as it allows you to determine if you are on the same page and feel comfortable with them. It is important to immediately address any concerns you have about your doctor or the hospital where they deliver babies. By doing so, you can determine whether to switch doctors, which is much easier to do early in your pregnancy.

To assist you in determining if your doctor is the right fit for you, I have compiled a list of the Top 20 Questions to ask them. These questions are frequently asked of doctors when they are witnesses in a case to get a better idea of how they practice. By asking these questions, you can gain insight into your doctor's approach to childbirth and better understand their experience, qualifications, and philosophy.

Top 20 Questions: Is Your Doctor Right for You?

1. How long has the doctor been practicing obstetrics, and approximately how many deliveries do they perform each year?
2. What percentage of your doctor's time is spent doing obstetrics versus gynecology? As an OB/GYN, your doctor is trained in both obstetrics, which is pregnancy-related, and gynecology, which encompasses other women's health issues.
3. Does the doctor's office have a fetal monitor to check your baby when needed?
4. At which hospital(s) does the doctor have privileges to deliver babies?

5. How long has your doctor had privileges at the hospital where you will deliver?
6. What level of care does the hospital(s) provide to baby after birth? (*see Chapter 5*)
7. How long does it take for your doctor to get to the hospital if they are at home or at the office? What about if it is rush hour?
8. Who will deliver your baby? Will it be your doctor or someone from their practice?
9. Does the doctor take call at the hospital where you are delivering? (*This is when they work a 12-hour shift at the hospital.*)
10. If residents or medical students will be part of your labor and delivery team, what is their role and how closely will they be supervised?
11. How well does your doctor work with the nurses and staff at the hospital where you will deliver?
12. Does the doctor have a good working relationship with the "in-house" doctors who may assist with your delivery if necessary?
13. Will the doctor come to the hospital to check on you when you are in labor, or do they just come in for the delivery?
14. When you are in labor at the hospital, does the doctor get updates from the nurse, midwife, or residents?
15. What if you do not like someone on your delivery team at the hospital? How should you handle this situation?

16. Can the doctor review your baby's heart rate remotely?
17. If so, will they review your baby's heart rate remotely without being called by a nurse or resident?
18. How does your doctor feel about C-sections versus vaginal deliveries?
19. At what point in labor will your doctor typically come to the hospital to assist with your delivery?
20. Inquire about any circumstances that may cause your doctor to be delayed or unavailable during your delivery, and who will take their place in those situations.

During your initial visit, these specific questions will shed light on what you can expect from your doctor and their approach to labor and delivery. If your doctor takes call at the hospital, it can be good news for you. In such a case, you may get lucky and have your doctor at the hospital during labor. Additionally, you can learn more about how your doctor will handle any issues that may arise with someone on your delivery team. Will your doctor be proactive and step in to make a change, come to the hospital, or choose to do nothing?

Another good question to ask is how quickly your doctor can arrive at the hospital if needed. This is especially important on busy days in labor and delivery when the in-house doctor may be tied up, and you may have to wait for your private doctor to arrive. Keep in mind that, unlike an ambulance, your doctor does not have lights and sirens to cut through traffic.

You should also inquire whether residents will be involved in your care and if your doctor trains them at the hospital. If a resident updates your doctor on your labor and raises concerns about your baby's heart rate, ask how your doctor will respond. Will they double-check the resident's interpretation, or do they trust them completely? Additionally, if you need a C-section, ask whether your doctor will perform it or supervise a resident. Residents learn to become doctors by practicing on moms like you, so find out what their involvement will be in your labor and delivery.

It is also important to find out which hospital your doctor delivers at and whether they have good after-birth care for your baby. For some moms with a higher risk delivery, this is very important.

Ideally, your doctor should have an excellent relationship with everyone at the hospital, and they should describe themselves as a "Dream Team" working together to deliver babies safely. If your doctor says anything negative about the nurses or residents at the hospital, this could be a red flag.

Another good thing to know is how many deliveries your doctor has done. Remember that while experience matters, it is not the only factor determining whether a doctor is good. Some newer doctors can be amazing, while some older doctors may make you feel uneasy. In the legal world, doctors being sued by moms come from a range of experience levels.

It is essential to remember that the Top 20 Questions to ask your doctor serve as a starting point for your conversation. Depending on how your doctor responds, you may want to follow up with additional questions or concerns specific to your situation. By gathering important information and addressing any concerns early on, you can make an informed decision about whether or not your doctor is the right fit for you.

Doctors at Trial

I have been in a trial with a doctor who was so overwhelmed about being sued by a family in a baby case that she could not drive herself to court. She literally could not drive a car from day one of the trial. She was a kind and hardworking doctor and this showed me firsthand the impact that these cases can have on doctors who are simply trying to provide the best care for their patient. It was a long trial, and her designated driver had a conflict a couple of evenings, so I would drop her off at home after the trial concluded for the day.

During the trial in downtown Detroit, held in December, the weather was exceptionally cold and snowy. Unfortunately, I realized that my boot heel had worn through to the metal stud only when I arrived in court one morning. As I walked around the courtroom, every step I took created a loud "ping" sound as the stud hit the hard floor. I tried my best to minimize the noise, but my efforts were futile, and it looked as though I was walking with a limp.

Later that night, as I drove the doctor home, she kindly offered to fix my damaged boot heel. She told me she knew someone who could fix my heel, so I handed her my boots and drove home in my socks.

Two days later, she arrived at court with both my boot heels fixed up like new. I was taken aback by her thoughtful act and thanked her. In response, she simply smiled and said that it was the least she could do. What stood out to me the most about her kind gesture was the fact that she was a highly respected doctor at the hospital. Despite her status, she went above and beyond to help me, which served as a powerful reminder of the kindness and generosity that some doctors possess.

The trial came to an end the Friday before Christmas. The jury was fully advised that the mother had no prenatal care, smoked marijuana during her pregnancy, presented to the hospital with vaginal bleeding and no amniotic fluid, and her baby's heart rate was poor upon arrival. It was a sad case for the baby, but we knew that whatever happened to the baby, it was before Mom arrived at the hospital. Regardless of these undisputed facts, the family got their Christmas verdict against the doctor and hospital that Friday. The jury awarded the family millions of dollars.

As we left the courtroom, a somber silence hung in the air. Heads down, we walked back to the office, stunned by the verdict. In the conference room, the doctor uttered the words that none of us wanted to hear: "I quit." It was clear that the verdict had shattered her, and she could no longer continue delivering babies at the hospital. In a matter of hours, we transitioned from being her legal representatives to her psychologists. We were not only disheartened by the verdict as her lawyers, but what was more upsetting was the impact it was having on the doctor and possibly her future. We emphasized that quitting her job would ultimately harm the mothers and families who needed her most. She was an exceptional and careful physician, one that any parent would trust to deliver their child. We devised a plan to appeal the verdict and requested that the doctor agree not to leave her position until the appeal was completed.

Several years later, justice was served when the appeal proved successful, and the verdict was overturned in favor of the doctor. The family and their attorney did not pursue another trial, nor should they have. Today, the doctor is still delivering babies and providing exceptional care to her patients.

Doctors understand that a mistake in their profession differs greatly from a mistake in other professions, which is why many of these doctors put their heart and soul into every delivery. The doctor from the trial was one such special physician who exemplified the best of the medical profession. These are the doctors who are deeply affected when a family accuses them of wrongdoing. They become paralyzed with sadness, especially when they know in their hearts that they did everything they could to help. They are the type of doctors that every parent would want to deliver their baby, and fortunately, there are many others who share the same level of compassion and expertise as the doctor in this case.

Chapter 5
Best Hospital for Baby

When it comes to hospitals, different levels of care are available for you and your baby. Higher-level hospitals offer specialized care that can be important if your baby requires any type of care after birth or is born prematurely. These hospitals have the resources and expertise to help your baby transition from life inside the uterus to life outside of it.

In rural areas, there may be limited options for hospitals. In some cases, you may not have any choice in which hospital you go to. There are usually more hospitals to choose from in larger cities and suburbs, including a mix of smaller and larger facilities. The size and number of hospitals in an area typically depend on the population size and the community's medical needs.

Choosing the right hospital for you and your baby is an important decision that should be made with careful consideration. You may need to weigh your options depending on your location and medical circumstances. This chapter will give you important information to consider when determining which hospital is best for you and your baby.

Level I Hospital: Basic Care Only in the Nursery

Level I hospitals are small community hospitals that typically have a basic newborn nursery. Pediatricians usually provide care to the baby after birth, and in some cases, the pediatrician may be on-call, which means they may be up to 30 minutes away from the hospital. Level I hospitals are not equipped to care for infants under 35 weeks' gestation or those requiring specialized care. If your baby needs specialized care, they will have to be transported to a Level II or III hospital. This not only poses a challenge of separating the mom and her baby, but also introduces downtime during transportation, which may affect the quality of care that the infant receives.

If delivering at a smaller Level I hospital, find out if a surgeon, anesthesiologist, and pediatrician are on-site 24 hours a day or on-call, which means they are not at the hospital. It is also important to know if they are there only during the day and on-call at night. Keep in mind, to perform a C-section, you need a surgeon and anesthesiologist. If either of the doctors are on-call, there could be a 20- to 30-minute period where you have to wait for their arrival. If an emergency C-section is called, this can be a problem if the baby needs to be delivered ASAP. Finding this information out beforehand will help you determine if this is the type of hospital you are comfortable delivering your baby at.

Level II Hospital: Specialized Nursery

A Level II hospital is a healthcare facility that provides specialized care to newborn babies. It is equipped with a specialized nursery and staffed with neonatologists and neonatal nurse practitioners with expertise in newborn care. Additionally, Level II hospitals likely have hospitalists or pediatricians who are on-site at the hospital instead of being on-call. This means that they can provide immediate care to newborns in need.

Level II hospitals are equipped to care for babies born after 32 weeks of gestation and weighing more than 1,500 grams (3.3 lbs).

Level III Hospital: NICU

Level III hospitals provide highly specialized care for newborns in their neonatal intensive care units (NICUs). These units are staffed by a team of dedicated professionals, including neonatologists, neonatal nurses, and respiratory therapists, who are available around the clock to monitor and care for premature or critically ill infants. In addition, Level III hospitals can consult with specialized pediatric experts, such as neurologists and cardiologists, if needed to ensure the best possible outcomes for their tiny patients.

These hospitals are equipped with the latest technology, including advanced imaging equipment such as MRI, CT, and echocardiography, which allow doctors to quickly diagnose and treat any medical issues that may arise. With their specialized staff and cutting-edge equipment, Level III hospitals are uniquely equipped to provide the highest level of care for critically ill newborns.

Level IV Hospital: Specialized or Regional NICU

This is a Level III hospital with specialized surgeons available 24 hours a day. This facility is for the complex care of infants who are very sick.

Hospitals with Cooling Therapies

Cooling therapy is a medical intervention that is available in some hospitals for newborn babies. In cases where an unexpected medical complication occurs just before or during birth, cooling therapy can be used to prevent or reduce injury to the baby's brain. The procedure involves lowering the baby's body temperature, which causes their brain cells to "go to sleep" for approximately 72 hours. This gives the cells time to recover and can result in improved outcomes for the baby's brain function.

The effectiveness of cooling therapy depends on how quickly it is started after birth. Therefore, if your baby is at high risk for complications during delivery, it is important to consider delivering at a hospital that offers cooling therapy for newborns. This can increase the chances of a successful outcome, as the procedure can be started immediately after birth in the event of an emergency.

Cooling therapy is not available at every hospital. However, hospitals that offer the therapy also have specialized transport teams on-call. If your baby is born at a smaller hospital, near one that has cooling therapy, the transport team can quickly transfer your baby to the larger hospital that offers the therapy.

Determine the Risk to Baby When Choosing a Hospital

Choosing the right hospital for you and your baby is a significant decision when it comes to giving birth. One of the key factors to consider is the method of delivery you have chosen. Some delivery methods may carry a higher risk for your baby than others. For instance, if you are having an elective C-section at 39 weeks, you may not need to prioritize finding a hospital with a NICU or cooling therapy. However, if you are attempting a vaginal birth after C-section ("VBAC") with Pitocin induction, it may be more critical to choose a hospital that has these resources available in case of an emergency.

When choosing a hospital for delivery, it is important to consider your chosen delivery method and evaluate the associated risks to you and your baby. Understanding the risk levels to your baby will help you pick the right hospital.

To help expectant mothers choose the right hospital for delivery, I have created a simple chart that outlines the various delivery methods, associated risks to the baby, and the level of hospital you should consider discussing with your doctor. This guide is specifically designed for uncomplicated pregnancies and healthy patients who have no underlying medical conditions.

Delivery Method	Risk Assessment as to Baby Only	Hospital Level to Discuss with your Doctor
Elective C-section	Low Risk	Level I or II
Vaginal Delivery without Pitocin	Lower Risk	Level I or II
Preterm Delivery (greater than 35 weeks)	Medium Risk	Level II or III
Induction of Labor with Pitocin	Medium to High Risk	Level II or III
VBAC without Pitocin	Higher Risk	Level II or III
Preterm Delivery (32 to 35 weeks)	Higher Risk	Level II or III
VBAC with Pitocin	Highest Risk	Level II or III
Preterm Delivery (less than 32 weeks)	Highest Risk	Level III

* Please note that this chart is only meant to serve as a guide, and it is crucial that you speak to your doctor about your specific needs and concerns. Your doctor will be able to provide you with personalized recommendations based on your medical history and current health status.

Should You Pick a Hospital Before Choosing Your Doctor?

When it comes to delivering your baby, choosing the hospital before picking the right doctor may be something to consider. It is important to note that your doctor must have privileges at the hospital in order to deliver your baby there. If your doctor does not have privileges at a particular hospital, then they cannot deliver your baby at that hospital.

If you are currently being treated by a doctor who delivers at a smaller hospital and you have a higher risk delivery, it is important to have an open conversation with your doctor about the hospital where you will deliver your baby. A smaller hospital is not going to be properly equipped if your baby needs specialized care after birth. While your doctor may not want to lose you as a patient, they should understand the importance of delivering at the right hospital for you and your baby's safety.

Another thing to consider are hospital policies, which can present potential risks for both you and your baby. For example, in a particular small community hospital, doctors were not on-site during most labors. To address this issue when there was a high-risk delivery, the hospital implemented a policy requiring the delivering doctor to remain on-site at the hospital if their patient was a VBAC so a timely C-section could be done if necessary. However, this policy overlooked a significant detail: performing a C-section requires an anesthesiologist, who may be up to 30 minutes away from the hospital. Even if the delivering doctor is present, a C-section would still require waiting up to 30 minutes for the anesthesiologist to arrive. Given this situation, attempting a VBAC at this hospital would not be advisable, as a potential delay in accessing an anesthesiologist could lead to serious risks for both mother and baby in case of an emergency C-section.

Pro Tip

Ultimately, choosing the right hospital and doctor can make all the difference in ensuring a safe and healthy delivery. So, before choosing your doctor, it is important to do your research and find out which hospitals they have privileges at. You should also take into consideration any potential risks associated with the hospital's policies and procedures. By doing so, you can make an informed decision that puts the safety of you and your baby first.

Avoid Transferring between Hospitals

It is crucial to have a good understanding of the hospitals in your area in hopes that you can avoid transfers between them during the onset of labor, during labor, or after birth. Two stories emphasize the importance of avoiding transfers between hospitals for both the health of the baby and the emotional well-being of the mother.

In the first story, a mother arrived at a Level I hospital with contractions at just 28 weeks pregnant. While there, her water broke, prompting the hospital to transfer her to a nearby Level III hospital to ensure her baby would receive specialized care after birth. However, during the ambulance transfer, the baby's condition deteriorated due to the lack of fetal monitoring. When they arrived at the Level III hospital, doctors discovered that the baby's heart rate was dangerously low, and an emergency C-section was performed, but the baby had already suffered significant injury during transport as the heart rate was not monitored. Had the mother known to go directly to the Level III hospital just 10 minutes away, her baby could have been continuously monitored and delivered safely. Experts who reviewed the case concluded that if the baby was not transferred between hospitals, the baby would likely have been born healthy and gone on to live a normal life.

The second story highlights the emotional impact on the mother, even when the baby is okay. The mother was undergoing a Pitocin induction with a term pregnancy at a Level I hospital, and there were complications, so the baby was transferred to a Level III hospital by helicopter following birth. The Level I hospital tried to keep the mother at the hospital while they flew her baby with strangers in a helicopter, but she insisted, "no way." She met her baby at the other hospital shortly after giving birth. While her baby was okay, the experience was traumatic for the mother and deterred her from having another baby for years. The good news is she is now expecting her next baby, but will be delivering at a different hospital with more specialized care.

These stories make it clear that the transfer between hospitals can impact both you and your baby, and you should always try to set yourself up to avoid any negative consequences.

Chapter 6

Do I Need a Labor and Delivery Plan?

This chapter was written to help you prepare for labor and delivery. An LAD (labor and delivery) plan involves learning about labor and delivery, and preparing yourself to make important decisions ahead of time. Unlike planning a vacation, where you can choose the dates, destination, and activities, planning for labor and delivery is much more complex. Many variables can arise, and things can change quickly. While this unpredictability makes it challenging to plan, it is also why having an LAD plan is important.

Decisions before versus during Labor

Decision-making before labor versus during labor is much different. Before labor, you have time to think, do research, read a book like this one, and call or text people to get their thoughts in the comfort of your home. When you go into labor, you enter a different state of mind. Labor is one of the few times that it is acceptable to be in a lot of pain, and if you pass on the epidural, this pain can be intense. If you want to take the edge off the pain, you can take medication. While all of this is normal, your decision-making may be affected by these factors.

For this reason, a highly respected doctor explained that moms should be given all of their labor and delivery options before their labor even starts. The doctor from the legal case explained:

> Some would argue that when a patient is in labor, it is impossible to have them make a decision. If they are in pain, they are in the anxious moment. So the true decision-making would be that conversation that occurs before she gets to the hospital, before she is in labor. (*Expert Witness*)

The doctor has been delivering babies for decades, and his explanation is a reminder that you will have a lot going on during labor, not only physically but mentally.

An LAD Plan Is More than Just a Plan

While writing this part of the chapter, I received two text messages about a mom who was 35 weeks pregnant at the hospital in the labor and delivery unit.

The first text message was from my sister. The text message was sent at 11:38 a.m. and read, "The baby's heart rate started descending, and they want to do an emergency

C-section; mom is scared shitless." I did not see my phone light up, and this message went unread.

The next message is sent 5 minutes later at 11:43 a.m. and is surprisingly from the mom in labor. "This is Kelly's friend ... we are at the hospital, and they want to do an emergency C-section. She said you might be able to give us some clarification." I happened to pick up my phone that was on "do not disturb" at 11:46 a.m. and saw both messages for the first time. The first words out of my mouth were of grave concern. I frantically call the mom, and her phone went to voice mail. I sigh in relief as I assume that the mom has been taken back to the operating room for a C-section. Then, in a minute of complete disbelief, my phone rings and it is the mom calling me back.

I answer the phone, "Hello, is everything okay? Is the baby stable?"

She responds, "Yes, but the doctor still wants to do a C-section. She thinks my placenta may be abrupting." The fact that we were on the phone discussing abruption and emergency C-section downgraded the situation as it became clear that it was not a true emergency. I was still very concerned at that point.

If you say the words "placental abruption" and "emergency C-section" to a baby lawyer, you can expect this response. I apologized to her for what I was about to say, but I felt that this was the clarification that she needed to hear. "I know you are pregnant and at the hospital, but I have to tell you something that I do not think your doctors have communicated to you. If your placenta pulls away from your uterus or abrupts, your baby will not be getting the oxygen she needs to survive. Your delivery team may only have minutes to get her out before she becomes very sick. These are the babies that have cerebral palsy, developmental delays, or do not make it. This is not a risk you want to take if your doctor believes your placenta is abrupting."

We talked a bit more, and it became clearer that there was more of a concern for abruption, and the words "emergency C-section" came into play because if the placenta was abrupting she would need one. The conversation then focused on the risks of delivering a preterm baby versus the concern of placental abruption. After we hung up that day, the mom decided not to have the C-section as she was only 35 weeks pregnant, and instead ended up being discharged from the hospital. She got weekly testing to ensure her baby was doing okay, and she had a healthy baby girl weeks later.

This story serves as a powerful reminder that an LAD plan is more than just a plan. It is a tool to help you prepare for the unpredictable nature of pregnancy and labor and delivery. By creating an LAD plan, you can start considering various scenarios that may arise and make informed decisions in advance. You start thinking for the first time, "What if my doctor says the words 'emergency C-section'? What will I do or why would I need one?" As you think, research, and prepare your LAD plan, you marinate in these thoughts.

As part of preparing and even reading this book, you now understand that there may be some obstacles as a normal part of labor and delivery. The element of surprise that can catch you off guard is not nearly as bad as if you were hearing it for the first time in your life. In the story, the mom was caught off guard and had a hard time understanding everything her doctor was telling her. That element of surprise can inhibit your ability to stay focused and can make everything seem very overwhelming. To help minimize these feelings, it is like many other things in life: you must prepare.

LAD Plan and Your Doctor

Talking to your doctor about your LAD plan is vital to your decision-making and planning process. If you have questions or want to elaborate on anything with your doctor, this is the time. It is recommended that you have this conversation with your doctor before the third trimester to ensure that there is ample time to make any necessary adjustments to your plan or to seek a different doctor who aligns better with your preferences.

Creating an LAD plan provides valuable insight into your doctor's approach to labor and delivery and their beliefs regarding important aspects of the process. This information can help you determine if you feel comfortable with your doctor's approach and if they are a good fit for you. One example of a conversation you should have with your doctor when discussing your LAD plan is the possibility of an operative vaginal delivery. It is important to note that doctors have different preferences when it comes to using instruments, such as vacuums or forceps, during delivery. By discussing this topic with your doctor, you can learn more about their preferences and approach.

As a baby lawyer, I know the personal preferences of many doctors when it comes to vacuum versus forceps. I was taking a deposition of a doctor and he testified, "I'm a forceps guy, was trained with forceps." Another doctor liked forceps because they do not "pop off" like a vacuum. Another doctor had no preference, but if he was performing a vaginal delivery in the operating room, he would likely use the vacuum because it was kept in that room.

In addition to discussing their preference as to an operative vaginal delivery, a good doctor will also take the time to explain the risks and benefits of each option so you can plan accordingly. There are very important risks and benefits to using a vacuum versus forceps. For instance, a vacuum is not as traumatic to the vaginal area as forceps. However, if your baby is in trouble, forceps can be more reliable than a vacuum in getting your baby delivered quickly. These are things you should talk to your doctor about before labor and delivery, which is exactly what an LAD plan helps you do.

When you go into labor, keep in mind that your OB/GYN doctor may not be available to deliver your baby. Instead, other doctors in the practice may be on-call and responsible for your labor and delivery. Discussing your LAD plan with all the doctors in the practice is essential to ensure that they are familiar with your preferences. Additionally, it is crucial to understand their preferences as well. This will help everyone be on the same page for your labor and delivery.

LAD Plan and Your Delivery Team

When you arrive at the hospital, your delivery team will perform an initial assessment and create a plan for your labor and delivery. The delivery team understands the importance of having a plan, which is why it is one of the first things they do when you arrive at the hospital. This is the time when you can provide your LAD plan to the delivery team, which will help them clearly understand your preferences and expectations during labor and delivery. Having this plan in place can help avoid miscommunication from the beginning and ensure that your team is on the same page. This could also prompt your delivery team to ask you questions to better understand your preferences.

When you arrive at the hospital, giving your LAD plan to your delivery team will show that you have prepared and thought carefully about your labor and delivery. This can set you apart from other expectant mothers who may not have a plan. By communicating your plan, you show your team that you are knowledgeable and involved in the process. This can improve communication and create a sense of partnership between you and your delivery team.

No LAD Plans in Legal Baby Cases

In legal baby cases, the labor and delivery plan created by the delivery team often becomes a point of contention. Whether the original plan was flawed or the mother should have been presented with different options that could have changed the plan, something went wrong. Ultimately, the plan failed the family in some way. As a result, attorneys for the families will carefully review the plan with the delivery team during their depositions in legal cases. They will ask questions about how the plan was developed, what the basis for the plan was, whether other options were presented to the mother, and so forth.

In the legal cases, families arrive at the hospital without a LAD plan, relying instead on the delivery team to provide them with information and recommendations. This approach often leaves mothers making important decisions on the spot, based on limited information provided by just one or two people. As a result, it is common for mothers to testify that they "did not know." Often times, if the doctor had given the mother different options or, in some cases, mom chose a different option in labor and delivery, then she never would have met someone like me. She would have no idea that people like me exist in this world. It is likely that when you first heard the words "baby lawyer" in this book and learned that we have been around a long time, you were probably learning something new. The bottom line is that moms want to make the right decisions during childbirth and as part of that, you must prepare so you can make informed decisions.

When to Write the LAD Plan

Congratulations, you are pregnant! You just took a pregnancy test and shit just got real. This is not an ideal time to write your LAD plan. Be pregnant for a while, enjoy it.

At or around 24 weeks' gestation, your baby reaches viability. This means your baby can now live outside of you under the right circumstances. This would be a good time to start thinking about your LAD plan. While you may already be running different plays in your head of how you might handle certain decisions, it is time to put pen to paper.

During pregnancy, there are many exciting things to look forward to, such as setting up your baby's nursery and shopping for cute clothes and diapers. However, it is important not to overlook one of the most vital aspects of pregnancy: preparing for childbirth. While it is natural to focus on the fun and exciting aspects of having a baby, creating a well-thought-out LAD plan should also be on your to do-list.

What to Put in Your LAD Plan

There is no one-size-fits-all LAD plan, and what someone may include in theirs may not be necessary for you or another person. Every pregnancy and patient is unique, so plans will vary from mom to mom. Labors are different for each mom, and you may have to make decisions that another mom does not. It is important to tailor your plan to your individual needs and preferences.

It is also important to remember that your LAD plan will evolve as you gain more information and experience throughout your pregnancy. Do not be afraid to ask questions, seek guidance from your doctor, and make adjustments to your plan as necessary. The process of creating a LAD plan can take weeks to months as you prepare yourself for childbirth.

A good starting point for creating your LAD plan is to consider your comfort level with medical interventions during labor and delivery. Medical interventions can include an epidural for pain or using Pitocin to induce contractions. These interventions are the opposite of natural, as your doctor is intervening in some way. For example, your water may break naturally, or your doctor may intervene and break it.

The type of interventions you may have to decide on during labor depends on your individual circumstances. Some women may be comfortable with a C-section if necessary, while others may prefer to exhaust all other options before considering one. As explained in the introduction, Sam did not want anything to do with a C-section unless it was absolutely necessary. I would later ask her why she was so against a C-section during her labor, and her response was simple: "Ewww, gross, a cut across my belly. No thanks." She literally just hates surgical incisions, as it grosses her out.

To help you kick-start your LAD plan, I have created a list of the top 10 things you should consider. Although there are numerous factors to think about, this list should serve as a good starting point.

Top 10 Things to Consider When Preparing an LAD Plan

1. Which type of fetal monitor would you prefer—external, internal, or wireless? *(Refer to Chapter 8 for more information.)*
2. Do you prefer continuous fetal monitoring or intermittent fetal monitoring? *(Refer to Chapter 8 for more information.)*

3. Do you want an ultrasound performed at the beginning of labor to make sure the baby is head down, check your amniotic fluid, and to estimate their weight?
4. Would you like to consider an epidural for pain relief?
5. Are you comfortable with the use of Pitocin to stimulate your contractions?
6. If you are okay with using Pitocin, what specific parameters would you like in place to ensure a safe induction of labor? *(Refer to Chapter 14 for more information.)*
7. Are you comfortable with the doctor breaking your bag of water or is this something you prefer to happen naturally?
8. If the baby can be safely delivered by C-section or operative vaginal delivery, which one do you prefer?
9. If an operative vaginal delivery is necessary, do you prefer the use of forceps or a vacuum?
10. Are you comfortable with the possibility of an episiotomy, or would you prefer to avoid one?

You can include many different things in your LAD plan beyond what is covered in this book. For example, you may want to consider different labor positions, using a birthing ball, or other comfort measures to manage pain. Additionally, you may want to consider preferences for after-birth care, such as breastfeeding or circumcision (if applicable). A couple that I found important are as follows:

- Do you have any preferences for the care of the placenta after birth?
- Do you want your partner to cut the umbilical cord?
- Do you want to have delayed cord clamping *(waiting a specific amount of time before cutting the cord)*?
- Do you want your baby to receive a Vitamin K injection at birth?
- Do you want your baby to receive eye ointment *(prophylaxis for bacterial infection)* after birth?
- Do you want your baby to receive the hepatitis B vaccine at birth?

Lastly, it is important to note that you can include any additional information or statements that you feel are important in your LAD plan. For example, if you have designated someone to be your baby advocate, you can include their name in the plan and the following statement:

- I give permission for the delivery team to discuss with my baby advocate my care during labor and delivery, the progress of my labor, and the well-being of my baby during labor and delivery.

Additionally, you can explicitly state that you want to be educated about all your medical options from admission until hospital discharge, so you can make informed decisions. Ultimately, your LAD plan should reflect your preferences and include any other information you feel is important for your healthcare providers to know.

It is important to remember that your birth plan is not set in stone. For example, if you initially decide that you do not want an epidural but then find yourself in more pain than you anticipated, it is okay to change your mind. Similarly, if a doctor suggests an intervention you had not planned for, they may do so with your and your baby's best interests in mind. It is important to remain flexible as part of the planning process. This should be easy—as discussed earlier in this chapter, part of the reason you are planning is to prepare you to pivot and adapt quickly to any unexpected changes or challenges during labor.

This chapter is an important starting point for preparing for labor and delivery. As you read through the rest of the book, consider the various decisions you may need to make and how you will approach them when the time comes. You may choose to develop your plan as you read, or take notes and create a plan afterwards. Regardless of the approach you take, the act of thinking through possible decisions can be incredibly beneficial in helping you feel more confident and prepared for childbirth.

Chapter 7
The Baby Advocate

As an attorney, I often find myself in the role of a "baby advocate" when speaking with friends and family about their pregnancy and childbirth. While I am not a medical professional and cannot offer medical advice, I can provide insights from the legal side of labor and delivery to help inform parents of the decisions that prioritize the safety of their baby.

In my role as a baby advocate, I always consider the potential risks associated with each decision made during labor and delivery. Even if the risk of harm to the baby is deemed low by medical professionals, it is essential to understand what that risk is and whether it is one you are willing to take. While rare, the consequences of even a small risk can significantly impact you and your baby's life. For this reason, it is important not to downplay the potential risks associated with each decision during labor and delivery.

One risk many moms face is whether they should try a vaginal delivery after a C-section. My cousin had to make this decision with her second baby. While Ali had attempted a vaginal delivery with the first baby, it ended in a C-section. During the prenatal visits for her second pregnancy, her doctor recommended that she try a vaginal delivery. The risk of doing a vaginal delivery after a C-section is a uterine rupture. This is when the uterus tears open in the area where the prior C-section incision was made. This is extremely bad for both the mom and her baby.

Ali called me after having this discussion with her doctor during the pregnancy. She was considering a vaginal delivery, given how adamant the doctor was that this was a safe option that plenty of moms have chosen with no problems. We went over the risk of uterine rupture and what that would look like for her baby if this occurred. My cousin's instincts told her C-section, so I did not feel like I had to say much during that initial conversation.

Ali went back and told her doctor that she wanted a C-section. The doctor said that repeat C-sections are done on a case-by-case basis. She would not schedule Ali for a C-section at 39 weeks and told her, "Let's see what happens."

Ali's water broke at 35 weeks, and she headed to the hospital. It was decision time. The doctor pushed for a vaginal delivery that would be jumpstarted with Pitocin. She asked Ali, "Why would I do a C-section on you if you are already going into labor?"

My cousin told her she was worried about the risk of a uterine rupture, to which the doctor responded that was a very low risk and vaginal delivery was a safe option for her and her baby.

After talking to her doctor at the hospital, Ali called me. She explained that her doctor wanted her to try a vaginal delivery, not a C-section. We talked for a bit; my discussion with her was much different that day than the one she had with her doctor. It was time to go down main street. I reminded her how bad uterine ruptures are if they occur and the risk to her and her baby. I explained, "If your uterus ruptures in labor and delivery, your doctor has to get the baby delivered within 8 to 10 minutes, or your baby may go too long without oxygen, not to mention the fact that you could die if your uterus ruptures. There is no way for your doctor to know if a vaginal delivery is a safe option, as she cannot physically see your uterus and make that assessment. The doctor has no idea how your uterus healed from the prior C-section, as your uterus is inside you. Plus, this is not the doctor who performed your C-section."

While my primary concern was the uterine rupture, Ali was having a hard time with the reason given her doctor's "low-risk" response as she pushed for a vaginal delivery.

The discussion went further. I reminded her she was pushing 40 years old, so why risk the vaginal trauma that can be associated with a natural birth when she had already had a C-section? Your vagina does not bounce back like it would in your early 20s. Also, the second C-section is far easier to recover from. The surgeon goes back through the same incision, lined with scar tissue, and recovery is less painful and much faster. I reminded her that her first labor was long and hard and ended in a C-section. I said everything that came to mind in the 10-minute window I had to lay out my case. At the end of the talk, I said my big word, which means there is no other option through my legal eyes: "If it was me, I would 'unequivocally' do a C-section." While on the phone, she did not commit to a decision; I could tell that her instinct was still on the side of having a C-section.

After we hung up the phone, my cousin went against her doctor's advice and requested that her second baby be delivered by C-section. After her baby was safely delivered by C-section, the doctor approached my cousin and told her something we both would never forget. She said that upon entering her abdomen, she could see the baby in the uterus through her prior C-section scar. She described that area of the uterus as paper thin with her baby's hair starting to poke through the old incision. The doctor told her that if she had tried a vaginal delivery, she would have suffered the unimaginable uterine rupture. The doctor thanked Ali for choosing to have a C-section that day. Had Ali followed her doctor's advice, the outcome of her baby and her life may have been much different. While the doctor was ready to take those risks associated with a uterine rupture, luckily, Ali was not.

After speaking with Ali about her experience, I knew her story needed to be shared with other moms. As we discussed including her story in this book, she revealed something that sent chills down my spine, making this story not only important, but crucial for other moms to hear. When I asked her if she would have chosen a vaginal birth had we not talked, she responded with a resounding, "Yes." Despite her preference for a C-section, her doctor pressured her to deliver vaginally by citing how many other mothers had done so without any complications. This made Ali feel like she was making a poor decision. In the end, Ali made the right choice for herself and her baby that day by going against the advice of her doctor and opting for a C-section. Her story serves as a compelling reminder that the best choice is not always the most common one recommended by your doctor. It also highlights the significance of having a baby advocate to help navigate these decisions.

Pro Tip

One important lesson to learn is that the "low-risk" scenario must be carefully evaluated against the potential danger to both the mother and the baby. It is essential to inquire why your doctor considers a particular course of action safe. Are they making assumptions based on likelihood, or do they possess concrete evidence that a particular method is safe for you and your baby? In Ali's situation, the doctor was not entirely sure if vaginal delivery was a safe choice and simply cited the low incidence of uterine rupture.

Your Baby Advocate

Your baby advocates are the people you choose to have by your side during your child's birth. They are typically the ones you love and trust the most. Having someone you trust to support you and prioritize your baby's safety can help alleviate some of the stress and anxiety that comes with childbirth.

While you focus on the physical and mental demands of bringing your baby into the world, your baby advocate can provide a sense of calm and reassurance.

In the case of my niece's labor, her mom, Kelly, was her baby advocate. Despite not having a medical degree or certification, Kelly had given birth to five children and knew what to expect. However, what made her the perfect baby advocate that day was her indescribable excitement. Soon, she would witness her first-born child holding her first grandchild as she remembered the powerful feeling of holding Sam for the first time. That love and excitement as the circle of life played out fueled her to be the best advocate she could be.

The importance of having a baby advocate cannot be overstated. These are the people who are closest to you, who know you best, and who will always have your back. They are the ones who will support you through every step of the labor and delivery process, providing you with the guidance and encouragement you need to make the right decisions for yourself and your baby.

As the circle of life continues to turn, it is important to remember that the bond between a mother and her child is one of the most powerful forces in the universe. Having a baby advocate who understands and appreciates that bond can make all the difference in the world. So, when it comes time to welcome your own little bundle of joy into the world, make sure you have a baby advocate by your side. They will be your rock and support system, helping you navigate this exciting and life-changing journey.

The Remote Baby Advocate

In cases where your baby advocate cannot be present, communication will be key. In today's digital age, staying in touch with someone is easy, even if they are miles away. Phone calls, text messages, and video chats can be used to stay in contact and provide updates on the progress of labor. One thing to remember is that hospitals can have poor cell phone service or Wi-Fi, so it is important to find out how you will communicate with your remote baby advocate ahead of time. This may involve finding out if the hospital has Wi-Fi available or if you will need to use a landline phone to stay in touch. Knowing the communication options available ahead of time will help prevent any unexpected communication issues during labor and delivery.

The stories in this book where I was personally involved, I never stepped foot in the hospital. Even though I was not there physically, I was able to communicate effectively with the mother or the designated baby advocate to help them understand important information. Do not underestimate the value of having someone in your corner, even if they cannot be there in person.

Preparing Your Baby Advocate

As your due date draws near, it is important to consider who will be present at your delivery and designate someone as your baby advocate. However, simply naming a family member or friend as the baby advocate is not enough. If you had never read this book, they would take on their normal role as a loving family member or friend who just wants the best for you and your baby. But now that you have read this book, why not take them to the next level?

Now that your baby advocate has a new job during your labor and delivery, they should get prepared, similar to someone starting a new job. If you start a new job that you have never done before, you will likely be trained to improve your performance and effectiveness. Equally important is ensuring your baby advocate is ready for their new job. Once they are prepared and know how to be a good advocate, this, combined with their love and excitement for your new baby, will make them the best advocate.

To be an effective baby advocate during labor and delivery, it is essential to have a firm grasp of the key factors. By understanding the five essential elements that make up a good baby advocate, they will be better equipped to advocate for your baby and make sure they are safely delivered.

#1 Discuss Your LAD Plan

As part of choosing your baby advocate, it is important to make sure they know what you are thinking. Sharing your LAD plan with your baby advocate is a critical step. Your baby advocate must have a clear understanding of your preferences and expectations for the birth of your baby, as well as the reasoning behind them. This information allows them to advocate effectively on your behalf.

One important reason to share your birth plan with your baby advocate is to allow them time to prepare. If you have specific desires, such as elective labor induction, your baby advocate needs time to research and plan accordingly. They can then give you the support you need to make informed decisions throughout the labor and delivery process.

Another reason to share your LAD plan is to prevent potential disagreements or misunderstandings between you and your baby advocate. By discussing your plan in advance, you can work together to resolve any conflicts and ensure everyone is on the same page. This open communication can also help build trust and strengthen your relationship, so you can approach your birth experience with confidence and peace of mind.

#2 Know the Art of Effective Communication
A baby advocate's ability to communicate effectively with the delivery team is critical to ensuring a successful labor and delivery. Whether navigating through triage or responding to changes in your baby's heart rate, they must be able to convey your preferences and concerns to the right people and facilitate change. This requires a delicate balance of being respectful and firm, while also remaining calm and composed in the face of potential disagreements.

In order to communicate effectively, a baby advocate must be able to listen actively and ask the right questions. They must also be able to convey information clearly and confidently, without resorting to demands or rudeness. By maintaining a calm and respectful demeanor, they can work together with your delivery team to ensure the best possible outcome for you and your baby.

#3 Provide Air Support for Good Decision-Making

A good baby advocate is an essential ally during labor and delivery, as they can provide valuable support and guidance when making critical decisions about the safe delivery of your baby. They can help you understand the potential benefits and risks associated with different options presented to you during labor. By helping you weigh the pros and cons of each decision, a good baby advocate can ultimately help you achieve the safest and healthiest delivery for you and your baby.

#4 Be Familiar with Fetal Monitoring

Your baby advocate should have a good understanding of how to interpret your baby's heart rate during labor and delivery. Although interpreting a baby's heart rate may seem intimidating at first, it is not rocket science and can easily be understood by non-medical persons who are open-minded and willing to learn. Spending a couple of hours learning about the basics of fetal heart monitoring can take the pressure off you. Likewise, they should be familiar with the different types of fetal monitors and how they function. Therefore, it is highly recommended that your baby advocate understands Chapters 8 and 9 in this book.

#5 Understand the Common Facts in Legal Baby Cases

Understanding the common issues or facts in legal baby cases can empower your baby advocate to ask the right questions or get clarification if they notice something does not seem right. When advocating for your baby, they are drawing upon their experiences and knowledge, so giving them the power of information will make them a stronger advocate for you and your baby.

It is important to highlight the potential consequences of not equipping your baby advocate with this knowledge. Without understanding the common mistakes or facts in legal baby cases, your advocate may miss important details or fail to recognize warning signs. This could result in a failure to advocate effectively on behalf of your baby.

Your baby advocate should go over Chapter 11 to review the common facts and issues in legal baby cases.

Chapter 8

Monitoring Your Baby during Labor: The Gold Standard

This chapter is a must-read for every expecting parent, as it provides valuable information about the different types of fetal monitors used to record your baby's heart rate. These monitors are used to graph the heart rate in various locations within the hospital, including next to your bed, and remotely so that doctors can review it anywhere. While each monitor has its own set of advantages and disadvantages, it is crucial to understand that the wrong monitor at the wrong time can result in your delivery team lacking important information about your baby's well-being. Therefore, it is vital for every expecting parent to understand the differences between the monitors so they can make an informed decision during labor and delivery.

The good news is that there are only three types of fetal monitors, making this chapter relatively short but informative. By the end of this chapter, you will have a better understanding of the types of fetal monitors available and how they work.

External Monitor: The Easiest

The external monitor is the traditional method for monitoring the baby's heart rate and contractions during labor. It involves placing a large strap over the mother's belly. This type of monitor is convenient because it can be used before your water breaks and does not require internal placement.

The application of an external monitor is also relatively simple, although it must be removed if the mother needs to use the bathroom or move around. However, the external monitor is less accurate than internal monitoring methods, particularly if the mother has a larger body type or if the baby is positioned in a way that makes it difficult to obtain accurate readings.

Internal Monitor: Gold Standard

The use of an internal monitor is considered the most accurate and reliable way to monitor both the baby's heart rate and the mother's contractions during labor. This involves the placement of two parts: a fetal scalp electrode to monitor the baby's heart rate, and an intrauterine pressure catheter (IUPC) to assess the strength and duration of contractions within the uterus.

After the amniotic sac ruptures, the fetal scalp electrode is inserted to obtain accurate readings of the baby's heart rate. This electrode is a small coil that is gently attached to the baby's scalp. The fetal scalp electrode then transmits information about the fetal heart rate through a wire that connects to the fetal monitor and then graphs on the monitor next to your bed. With this device, the medical team can get precise and real-time information about the baby's heart rate, which helps them monitor the baby's health and respond accordingly.

The intrauterine pressure catheter (IUPC) is a highly precise method of evaluating the strength, duration, and frequency of contractions during labor. It measures the pressure inside the uterus, providing a more accurate assessment than external methods. The IUPC is a catheter that is inserted inside the uterus and measures changes in pressure as the uterus contracts. This is why you can see the small hills on the fetal monitor during contractions—they represent the increase in pressure inside the uterus. As the contraction ends, the pressure returns to the baseline or the resting tone.

During my conversation with Sam about her experience with an internal fetal monitor, she shared that it "felt weird." It is essential to understand that this type of monitor involves a wire being attached to the baby's head and then connecting to the mother's leg and a monitoring machine. While it may not be the most comfortable option, it provides accurate and dependable information on the baby's heart rate, which can be key in ensuring the baby's well-being during labor.

Wireless Monitor: New Technology

The Monica Novii Wireless Patch System, also known as Novii, is the latest type of monitor that allows expectant mothers to walk around during labor. With a range of up to

100 feet, the wireless monitor enables moms to stay mobile while the device picks up their baby's heart rate. The Novii system consists of five adhesive patches or electrodes and a pod that are affixed to the mother's belly. The electrodes are responsible for detecting the baby's heart rate, the mother's heart rate, and contractions. Bluetooth technology then transmits the information to the Novii device, which is then displayed on the fetal monitor.

The wireless monitor is a type of external fetal monitor. While it provides the mother convenience and freedom of movement, it is not as precise or reliable as an internal monitor. One drawback of the wireless monitor is that signals can be lost, which leads to the baby's heart rate no longer graphing. The nurse must troubleshoot the issue to reestablish the signal when this happens. This can lead to delays and disruptions in monitoring the baby.

Legal Cases: Internal Monitor versus the Wireless Monitor

It is important to note that both internal and wireless monitors have their own advantages and limitations. While an internal monitor is hard-wired to your baby and provides a continuous and accurate heart rate reading, it is considered a more invasive method, as it involves attaching the electrode directly to the baby's scalp. On the other hand, a wireless monitor is non-invasive and can be used earlier in labor, before the water breaks, and can allow the mom to walk around. However, it may lose or drop the signal of the baby's heart rate and provide a less accurate reading of it during labor.

While wireless monitors can be convenient and non-invasive, there have been a number of legal cases where wireless monitors were used during labor. In each case, the baby's heart rate was graphing, then something happens in the baby's environment, and the baby gets into trouble. The wireless monitor starts to lose the delicate signal of the baby's heart rate instead of showing that the baby is in trouble (like an internal monitor would do). The delivery team will start troubleshooting the wireless monitor to get the fetal heart rate to graph, and these steps take time. Ultimately, in each case, they could not get the baby's heart rate back on the wireless monitor, so other methods were used to find the heart rate, which took more time. In every case, the baby was in serious trouble, and an emergency C-section was eventually performed. Due to the length of the delay in all these cases, from troubleshooting the wireless monitor and setting up a different way to check the baby's heart rate, all the babies passed away either before or after birth.

The legal cases involving uterine ruptures demonstrate the critical difference between internal and wireless monitors. In one case where an internal monitor was used, the drop in the baby's heart rate was immediately apparent after the uterus ruptured, and the medical team was able to act quickly and deliver the baby, saving their life. However, in the other case where a wireless monitor was used, the monitor failed to detect that the baby was in trouble after the uterus ruptured and instead began losing the wireless signal. Only sporadic snapshots of the baby's heart rate could be seen on the monitor. The delivery team spent precious time troubleshooting the wireless monitor and trying to find the baby's heart rate before an ultrasound finally revealed that the baby was in trouble. The length of time that it took to determine that the baby was struggling resulted in the baby passing away.

Pro Tip #1

Expecting mothers can learn a valuable lesson from these two cases. Using an internal monitor during labor may seem invasive, but it provides accurate and reliable data on the baby's heart rate, allowing the delivery team to take quick action if necessary. In contrast, a wireless monitor can lose the baby's delicate heart rate signal, potentially delaying delivery and putting the baby's health at risk. Therefore, opting for an internal monitor may result in a faster delivery if complications arise.

Pro Tip #2

In legal baby cases involving wireless monitors when the infants did not survive, the labors were induced by Pitocin. To ensure your baby's safety during labor, consider requesting an internal monitor if Pitocin is used during your labor.

Doppler or External Monitor: Intermittent Monitoring during Labor

Continuous monitoring of a baby's heart rate is a standard procedure in most hospitals across the United States. This is because changes in heart rate can indicate that the baby is in trouble. By watching the heart rate continuously, the delivery team can quickly identify any issues and provide options to improve the baby's condition or deliver the baby if necessary.

In contrast, intermittent monitoring involves checking the baby's heart rate periodically using a Doppler or an external fetal monitor. Typically, the delivery team will check the heart rate before, during, and after a contraction.

Some people believe that only intermittent monitoring should be done during labor. The reasoning is that continuous monitoring results in more unnecessary intervention. Plus, without the constraints of a monitor, Mom can walk around and easily change positions. She can use gravity to help naturally deliver her baby and allow the body to do what it is supposed to do.

In one legal case, a mother chose intermittent monitoring, not realizing the risks to her baby. During her deposition, she recalled that her doctor approached her during the pregnancy about delivering her baby and using only intermittent monitoring for her baby's heart rate. The doctor explained all the great benefits, and, as a first-time mom, she agreed to only have her baby's heart rate checked once in a while during labor. Unfortunately, her baby experienced complications that were difficult to detect due to the intermittent monitoring. When the delivery team noticed that the baby was struggling, they quickly performed an emergency C-section, but unfortunately, a very sick baby was born. The delay in delivering the baby was attributed to intermittent monitoring, and questions were raised about the purpose of this type of monitoring in the lawsuit.

The mother was understandably upset and testified that people were shocked that the doctor did not continuously monitor her baby's heart rate during labor. It became apparent from her testimony that she did not fully understand the risks associated with intermittent monitoring when the doctor presented the option to her. Instead, the mother learned after the delivery of her baby the importance of continually monitoring the baby's heart rate during labor.

Pro Tip
This case highlights the importance of continuous monitoring during labor to detect any potential issues with the baby's well-being. By consistently tracking the baby's condition, the delivery team can act quickly and safely to deliver the baby if necessary. On the other hand, intermittent monitoring may not provide sufficient information to identify potential problems, which could result in unnecessary delays and increased risks to the baby. Therefore, it is essential to understand the benefits of continuous monitoring, which can help ensure the safest possible delivery for your baby.

Which Monitor Should Be Used in Your Labor?

In legal cases involving babies, the type of fetal monitor used during labor can be a significant point of contention. There is a big difference in opinions among doctors, resulting in varying recommendations to moms during labor. Some doctors may choose not to use an internal monitor unless there are concerns about the baby's heart rate or there are issues with the external or wireless monitor graphing the baby's heart rate. In contrast, other doctors may take a more liberal approach to using an internal monitor due to its reliability.

When it comes to fetal monitoring during labor, it is important to have an open discussion with your doctor about the available options at the hospital, the potential benefits and risks, and your personal preferences. For instance, you may want to consider whether you prefer a more natural experience, such as moving around during labor, or if you would feel more at ease being connected to a machine that can quickly detect any potential issues with your baby's well-being.

When developing your LAD plan, including your preferences for fetal monitoring during labor is important. By incorporating your fetal monitoring preferences into your LAD plan, you can help ensure that your doctor is aware of your preferences and can make every effort to accommodate them during your labor and delivery.

Chapter 9

What You Need to Know about Your Baby's Heart Rate during Labor

The baby's heart rate on a fetal monitor is a crucial element in almost every legal baby case. This is because the mistakes made during labor and delivery often center around the baby's heart rate. As a result, analyzing the heart rate on the fetal monitor is one of the first skills that baby lawyers learn, and it is the first thing we review when a new case comes in. The baby's heart rate is a critical component of every case, as it indicates whether the baby is doing well or poorly during labor and delivery.

Just like in a legal baby case, your baby's heart rate on the fetal monitor is one of the most important parts of your labor and delivery. You will likely have to make decisions based on your baby's heart rate, regardless of whether it is good or bad. To prepare yourself to make good decisions, your baby's heart rate should be one of the first things you learn about.

This chapter will guide you on how to read your baby's heart rate on the fetal monitor, so you know how your baby is doing during labor. Additionally, it includes information I have learned from the legal baby cases, which will help you make good decisions and possibly make a difference in your own labor and delivery.

What Is the Fetal Monitor Showing?

The fetal monitor shows two graphs: one for your baby's heart rate and one for your contractions. The top graph shows your baby's heart rate in beats per minute (bpm), and you read it from left to right. Each line going up on the graph represents an additional 10 bpm, and the numbers on the graph represent different beats per minute, such as 90, 120, 150, and 180. The ideal range for your baby's heart rate is between 110 and 160 bpm. To find your baby's heart rate, look at the horizontal line on the graph and see where it intersects with the numbers. That number is your baby's heart rate in bpm.

The graph shows your baby's heart rate over time. Each straight up-and-down line represents 10 seconds of the heart rate, and every darker line that goes across the graph represents 1 minute of the heart rate. By counting the darker lines, you can quickly find out your baby's heart rate for the past 5 or 10 minutes.

What You Need to Know about Your Baby's Heart Rate during Labor

This is an example of a what a fetal monitor that graphs the baby's heart rate will look like.

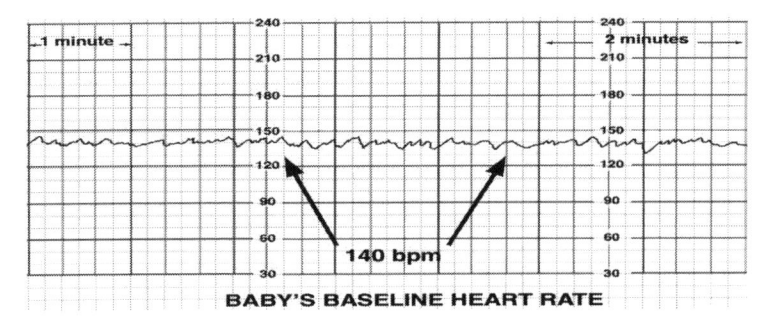

BABY'S BASELINE HEART RATE — 140 bpm

When looking at a fetal monitor, there are four aspects of your baby's heart rate that you must commit to memory. These include the baseline, accelerations, decelerations, and variability. Although these are medical terms, they are simple to understand and have common sense meanings, making them easy to remember.

Baseline: Normal Range 110 to 160 BPM

The baby's baseline heart rate is the horizontal line on the graph. A normal baseline is between 110 and 160 beats per minute (bpm). But there are two concerning types of baselines.

Bradycardia is when the heart rate goes below 110 bpm. This means that your baby might not be getting enough oxygen-rich blood. The doctors will try to increase the heart rate, and if that does not work, they might recommend delivering the baby. The delivery team should remain at your bedside until the lower heart rate is fixed or baby is born.

Tachycardia is when the heart rate goes over 160 bpm. There are different reasons for tachycardia, like infection or dehydration. But the most concerning reason is when the baby is having trouble and the heart rate beats faster to get baby more oxygen-rich blood. The doctors will try to lower the heart rate or do tests to see how the baby is doing. They will also look at other aspects of the baby's heart rate like the variability. For instance, if the heart rate is fast but has good variability, it is better than if the variability goes from good to bad.

This is an easy example of a normal baseline, bradycardia, and tachycardia.

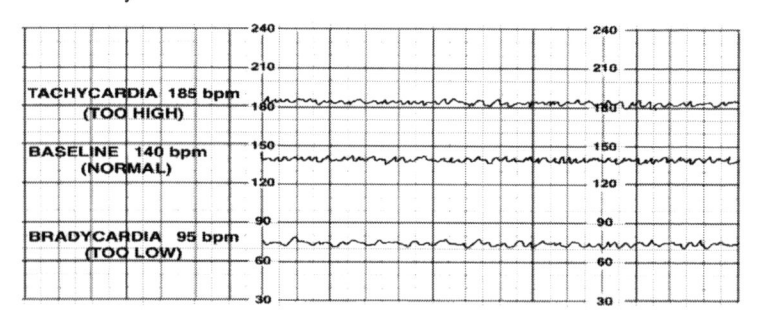

TACHYCARDIA 185 bpm (TOO HIGH)		
BASELINE 140 bpm (NORMAL)		
BRADYCARDIA 95 bpm (TOO LOW)		

To accurately determine a baby's baseline heart rate, the delivery team will monitor it for a period of 10 minutes and calculate the average rate. For instance, if the baseline heart rate is 140 beats per minute (bpm) and it drops down to the 120s for a sustained period of 10 minutes, this is considered a change in baseline. The new baseline rate is now considered to be 120 bpm. It is essential to note that the delivery team looks at 10-minute snapshots of the baby's heart rate to determine its baseline.

Variability or Fluctuations in the Baseline

Variability refers to the natural fluctuations in your baby's heart rate, which can be measured from the lowest to the highest point. While a healthy baby's heart rate may have a baseline of around 140 beats per minute (bpm), it is normal for it to fluctuate between 5 and 25 bpm. These are the quick up-and-down movements of the baseline.

There are four types of variability, each with descriptive terms that are easy to understand. Although there are associated numerical values, it is easy to determine the type of variability based on the appearance of the graph without getting too caught up in the numbers.

1. Absent: No fluctuations in the baby's heart rate. It is a straight line.
2. Minimal: Minimal fluctuations in the baby's heart rate. Close to a straight line with some minimal squiggles. It is 2 to 5 bpm.
3. Moderate: Moderate fluctuations in the baby's heart rate. It is between 5 and 25 bpm.
4. Marked: Huge fluctuations in the baby's heart rate over 25 bpm.

This is a graph demonstrating the different types of variability you could see on the fetal monitor. As you will see, the descriptive terms correlate with what you see on the graph.

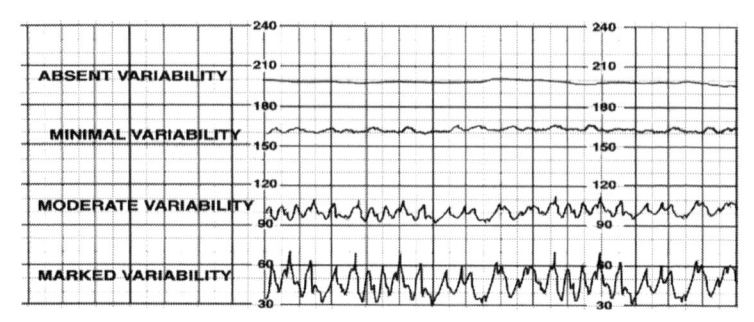

[Graph showing: ABSENT VARIABILITY (flat line), MINIMAL VARIABILITY (slight waves), MODERATE VARIABILITY (moderate waves), MARKED VARIABILITY (large waves), with y-axis values 240, 210, 180, 150, 120, 90, 60, 30]

To ensure that your baby is doing well during labor, it is important to understand the significance of the different types of variability on the fetal monitor.

Moderate Variability

Committing moderate variability to memory is key, as this is what you want to see. Moderate variability means your baby is likely well-oxygenated and doing great.

Minimal Variability

Minimal variability could indicate that your baby is either struggling, possibly napping, or other reasons depending on your labor. However, the most important reason for minimal variability that you must be aware of is whether it means your baby is starting to struggle. If you see minimal variability, you must also look at what else is going on with the baby's heart rate. If there are other concerning changes in the heart rate, such as tachycardia (higher heart rate) or decelerations (short decreases in the baby's heart rate), along with the minimal variability, this could be a cause for concern. While the significance of this depends on your specific labor, it is crucial to notify your delivery team of these changes if they are not already at your bedside. Your team can perform tests to check on your baby or interventions that will help improve your baby's oxygenation, which, in turn, should help get the variability back to moderate.

Absent Variability

I have only seen spurts of absent variability in legal cases. When this happens, there is usually a concerning heart rate with decelerations or bradycardia, and the delivery team is flying in to expedite delivery.

Marked Variability

When there is too much variability, it is called marked variability. I have encountered cases with marked variability, and there is no consensus on its significance. However, as a moderate variability snob, my Spidey senses would go up if this were my baby. It would be important to talk to your delivery team and get their input on the marked variability.

Interpreting Variability

It is important to keep in mind that interpreting variability is not an exact science, and different experts in legal baby cases have described the same variability differently. One doctor may say it is minimal variability, while another may call it moderate. If you have any questions about the type of variability graphing on the fetal monitor, do not hesitate to ask your nurse or someone on your delivery team for clarification.

The two most common types of variability are minimal and moderate. To help you understand the difference, each one has been placed on a graph for comparison. Notice how minimal variability is closer to a straight line, while moderate has more dramatic fluctuations.

MINIMAL VARIABILITY: STRAIGHTER LINE WITH MINIMAL FLUCTUATIONS

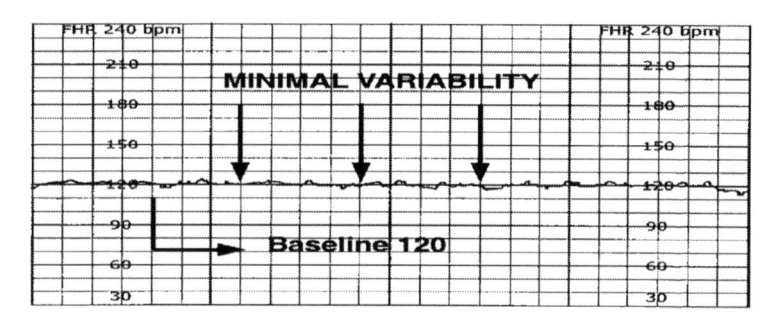

MODERATE VARIABILITY WITH FLUCTUATIONS BETWEEN 5 TO 25 BPM

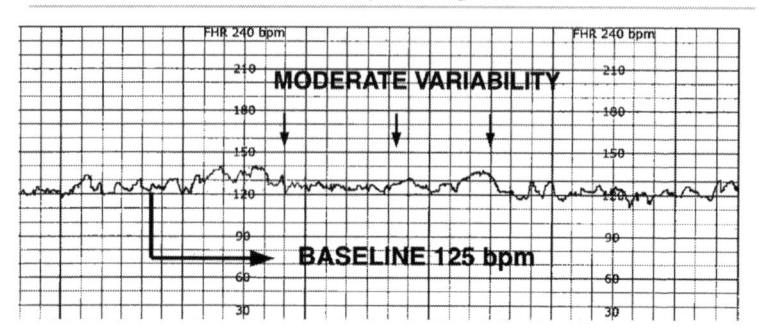

Accelerations in the Baby's Heart Rate

Commit accelerations to memory. These are a positive sign your baby is well-oxygenated. An acceleration is when the baby's heart rate increases for at least 15 seconds, resulting in a short spike above the average baseline. The rule of 15 x 15 applies here, meaning the heart rate increases by at least 15 bpm for at least 15 seconds.

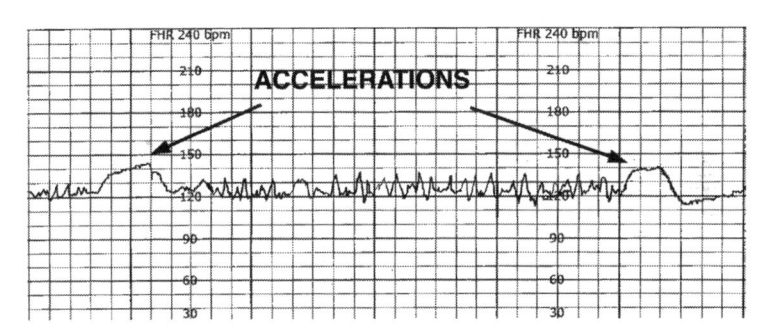

Decelerations in the Baby's Heart Rate

A deceleration is a decline or drop in the baby's heart rate from the baseline that lasts for a short period of time before the heart rate returns to the baseline. We often shorten the word to "decel" when discussing a baby's heart rate. Decelerations have their own characteristics, but it is important to consider the contractions to determine what kind of deceleration you are looking at. There are three types of decelerations:

1. Early Deceleration: Associated with the beginning of a contraction.
2. Variable Deceleration: They are variable, meaning will or will not be associated with a contraction.

3. Late Decelerations: Associated with the middle to the end of a contraction.

Early Deceleration

Early decelerations refer to a drop in fetal heart rate associated with the beginning of a contraction. These are generally considered benign and not a cause for concern in healthy pregnancies.

Variable Deceleration

Variable decelerations can occur independently or in association with a contraction, and they are characterized by an abrupt drop in fetal heart rate. The term "variable" also refers to the fact that the severity and duration of the decelerations can vary. Compression of the umbilical cord is one possible cause of variable decelerations.

While variable decelerations can be common in most labors, it is important to watch how often they occur and how long they last. If variable decelerations occur with every contraction or every other contraction or last longer than two minutes, your delivery team will be at your bedside, as there are interventions that can help stop or decrease the number of decelerations. However, there are no specific guidelines on the number of variable decelerations that require intervention, as it depends on the individual labor and your delivery team. Prior to the variable decelerations becoming frequent or lasting longer than two minutes, different delivery teams may respond to the variable decelerations differently.

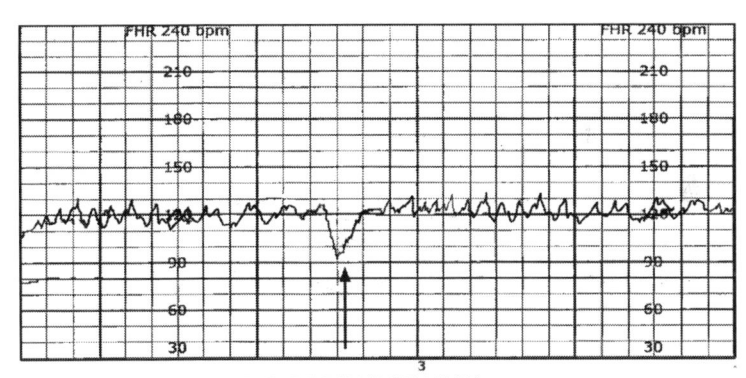

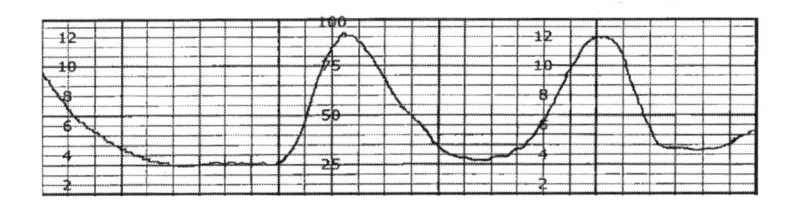

If there are variable decelerations in your labor, it is also important to look at other factors, such as the baby's heart rate variability and accelerations, to assess how they are doing. If the baby's heart rate variability is moderate and there are accelerations, this is a good sign that the baby is well-oxygenated. On the other hand, if the variability decreases to minimal and there are no accelerations, plus variable decelerations, this may be a cause for concern.

Below are two graphs demonstrating variable decelerations. The first graph shows a single variable deceleration, while the second graph shows a picture of two variable decelerations. The single variable deceleration would not be as alarming as the second graph with two variable decelerations.

SINGLE VARIABLE DECELERATION

VARIABLE DECELERATION

TWO VARIABLE DECELERATIONS HAPPENING WITH EVERY OTHER CONTRACTION

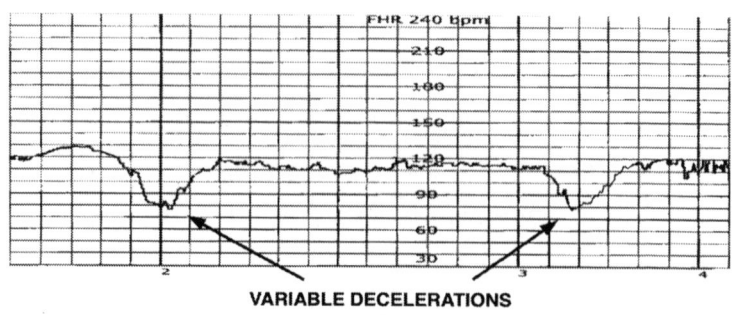

Late Deceleration

Late decelerations are a serious concern during labor, as they indicate that the baby may be struggling with oxygenation. This happens when the fetal heart rate slows down or gradually decelerates at the peak of a contraction. As the contraction squeezes the baby, their heart rate drops and slowly goes back up as the contraction becomes less intense. This suggests that the baby is having difficulty with the contractions, which may be related to how the placenta is functioning.

It is crucial to monitor how often late decelerations occur and how long they last, as they are the most concerning type of deceleration. If you experience late decelerations during labor, your delivery team should respond quickly to help the baby. Depending on the situation, they may intervene in different ways.

What You Need to Know about Your Baby's Heart Rate during Labor

The graph below demonstrates two late decelerations. If you see this pattern during your labor, your delivery team should be at your bedside to address the issue promptly.

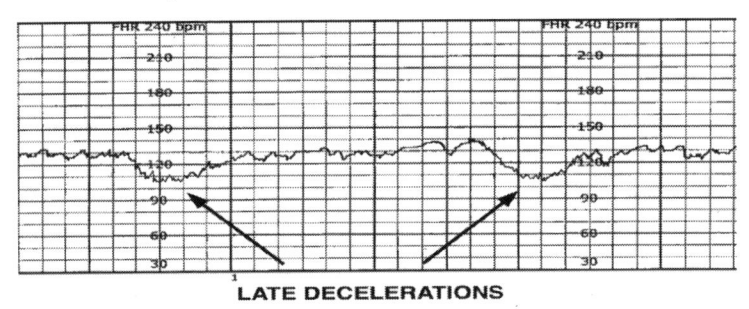

LATE DECELERATIONS

The Race Car Analogy

Picture yourself as an expert race car driver, equipped with exceptional training and skill. Your upcoming race presents a unique challenge: a ten-mile straight road track featuring orange cones staggered throughout the course. Your objective is to complete the race in under ten minutes, without colliding with any of the cones. Fortunately, only one driver will be on the track at any given time, allowing you to focus solely on your performance.

Your car's average speed during the race is the speed you need to maintain for 10 minutes to complete the track. To win the race, your speed must be between 60 and 65 mph—slower will not cut it, and faster will make you lose control. Similarly, your baby's heart rate has an average speed, measured in beats per minute (bpm). During labor, the speed of your baby's heart rate should stay between 110 and 160 bpm. If the baseline speed drops below 110 bpm, it is too slow and may indicate problems with finishing the race. If it goes above 160 bpm, it is too high or fast. The baby needs to slow down and stay in the normal range of 110 to 160 bpm to safely complete their race.

When driving the course, you may have the opportunity to accelerate for a short period until you approach a cone that requires you to maneuver around it. This can be beneficial if you can execute a quick acceleration, as it can help you complete the race faster and win. Similarly, if your baby's heart rate briefly accelerates during labor, this is a positive sign. It likely indicates that the baby is well-oxygenated and winning.

As a race car driver, you have the option to slow down or decelerate when faced with trouble while driving around the cones. If you slow down briefly to maintain control of your car, it may not affect your time significantly. However, continuing to decelerate or running off the road is a serious problem that can prevent you from winning the race. In such a scenario, changing your driving strategy is important to ensure you can complete the course in 10 minutes and win the race. Similarly, during labor, if your baby's heart rate continues to decelerate or decrease, it could indicate a problem that may make it difficult for the baby to reach their finish line or delivery. Unlike in the race, where the issue may be related to driving strategy, a slowing of the baby's heart rate could indicate a complication during labor.

Variability would be like maneuvering the race car around the cones as you drive from one side of the road to the other to avoid hitting them. If you are going to successfully complete the course, you cannot hit the cones. A bird's-eye view of your drive will show a zigzag pattern rather than a straight line down the road. Similarly, your baby's heart rate variability is when the baseline goes up and down or zigzags. The variability that you should see in your baby's heart rate is just like if you were completing the racetrack without hitting a cone. This is called moderate variability, which means it goes up and down within a healthy range. This likely indicates a well-oxygenated baby who is on track to win their race.

If you do not put enough effort into avoiding the cones and end up hitting most or all of them, it will almost look like a straight line down the road. This is a big problem because, besides likely being disqualified, you will not win your race. Similarly, if your baby's heart rate does not go up and down within a healthy range and instead appears as more of a straight line, this is called "minimal to absent variability." This can be concerning, as it suggests your baby may not be in a good position to get to their finish line. Just as it would be important to determine why you hit all the cones during a race, it is important to figure out why the variability of your baby's heart rate is minimal or more of a straight line.

To succeed in your race, you must maintain your average winning speed, briefly accelerate when possible, and avoid hitting cones. Similarly, to help ensure a safe delivery, your baby's heart rate must remain within the normal baseline range, occasionally accelerate, and show good or moderate variability. These factors are important for your baby to win their race to the outside world.

Categories for Your Baby's Heart Rate

In 2008, the medical community established categories for a baby's heart rate. You look at your baby's heart rate and place it in one of three categories. If patients knew about the categories, it would be an effective way to communicate how their baby is doing. Category I means your baby is a superstar with a normal baseline rate (110 to 160 bpm), moderate variability, accelerations, and no decelerations. Even if there are no accelerations, the tracing remains a Category I. Category III is the exact opposite of Category I. It indicates your baby is in trouble with absent variability, late or variable decelerations, or bradycardia. If you hear or see that your tracing is a Category III, your delivery team should be discussing C-section or operative vaginal delivery with you to get your baby delivered.

Category II is like the gray area of baby heart rate monitoring during labor. It is not as great as Category I, but not as concerning as Category III. If your baby's heart rate falls into Category II, it means some changes in the heart rate require close monitoring to ensure it does not deteriorate. Although it is common to see Category II in labor, your delivery team should closely monitor your baby and discuss any concerns or options with you.

When it comes to categories, your delivery team will keep you in the loop if they know you understand the categories. As your delivery team updates you on which category your baby's heart rate falls into, this is a guide on how your delivery team should be responding.

- Category I: Life is good and everyone is relaxed.
- Category II: Heightened sense of awareness. Watching the heart rate carefully for any changes. For instance, if there have been late decelerations, determine whether they are resolving (good) or becoming more frequent (bad).
- Category III: This is when things get intense. You may hear raised voices, see unfamiliar faces, and notice people moving quickly. Do not panic. Your delivery team is responding exactly as they should be.

The category system is a simple way for you to communicate with your delivery team. Once the fetal monitor has started, inform your nurse that you are familiar with the categories and request that they provide regular updates in case the baby's heart rate shifts to a different category. This will help with the communication between you and your delivery team.

As an example, below is a Category I graph, which means the baby is happy. Compare and contrast to the graph beneath it, which is Category II with minimal variability and decelerations.

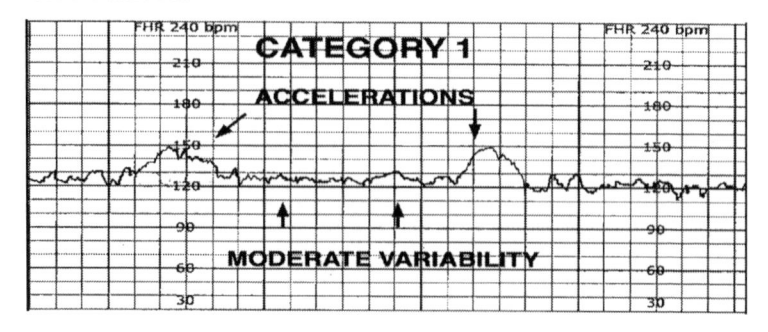

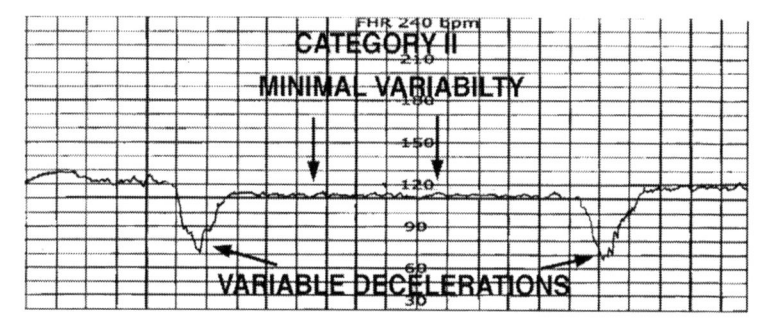

```
FHR 240 bpm                CATEGORY 1                    FHR 240 bpm
         210                                                   210
         180         ACCELERATIONS                             180
         150                                                   150
         120                                                   120
          90           ↑         ↑                              90
          60        MODERATE VARIABILITY                        60
          30                                                    30
```

```
                     FHR 240 bpm
                        CATEGORY II
                     MINIMAL VARIABILTY
                            ↓
                           150
                           120
                            90
                            60
                     VARIABLE DECELERATIONS
                            30
```

Doctors Do Not Agree on Interpretation of Baby's Heart Rate

In the legal realm of obstetrics, it is not uncommon for doctors and nurses to review fetal monitor tracings and have differing opinions about the baby's heart rate. One doctor may argue that the heart rate was concerning and that the baby should have been delivered by C-section earlier, while another will state that the baby was healthy and it was appropriate to continue with labor. What one doctor finds alarming about a baby's heart rate may not be concerning to another. Whether the baby is saying, "I am all good," or "Get me out of here," doctors do not always agree.

One expert witness explained that there are "still disagreements on a daily basis" as to what a baby's heart rate means. The expert brought examples of a baby's heart rate to the deposition because sometimes doctors "are just not even close to being right" about a baby's heart rate. This testimony has been echoed by many other experts who have testified in similar legal cases involving babies.

The Concerning Fetal Heart Rate in Legal Baby Cases

In my experience with baby cases, I have observed a consistent pattern of changes in the fetal heart that would indicate a baby is undergoing stress. Initially, upon admission to the labor and delivery, the fetal heart shows a reassuring tracing with a normal baseline, moderate variability, and accelerations. However, as labor progresses and the baby becomes stressed, I have noticed three distinct changes that occur in nearly every case. These changes can be described as follows:

1) A decrease in variability from moderate to minimal.
2) Variable or late decelerations start appearing on the fetal monitor and become more frequent, possibly prolonged.
3) Disappearance of accelerations.

When these changes occur, it is like a slippery slope, and, in many cases, the baby's heart rate becomes bradycardic or below 110 bpm. In legal cases, the delivery team starts to intervene, and eventually, delivery is expedited by C-section or operative vaginal delivery (vacuum or forceps). As these are baby cases, it means that the delivery was not timely because the infant sustained an irreversible injury.

The reality is that most doctors would likely be highly concerned if they received a phone call alerting them to the three changes in the baby's heart rate that I have observed. However, a significant problem arises in the interpretation of fetal monitor tracings. Even with the benefit of hindsight, doctors often disagree on the meaning of the same tracing. One expert may identify moderate variability and four decelerations, while another expert may view the same tracing and describe it as minimal variability with eight decelerations. Each interpretation has a different meaning, which means different recommendations or interventions.

One expert provided an excellent solution to this issue of varying interpretations, which is a straightforward and easy concept to grasp: When in doubt, err on the side of caution and give the baby the benefit of the doubt. It is better to be the one who describes the tracing as having minimal variability with eight decelerations than to be the one who characterizes it as having moderate variability with four decelerations. Depending on what else is going on in labor, the delivery team's recommendations could be different based on the different interpretations. A difference that could get your baby out of a bad spot or not.

One important takeaway from the conflicting opinions is that parents need to know how to read and discuss their baby's heart rate with their delivery team. It is worth noting that most nurses read the fetal monitor tracing much closer than the doctors. In my experience, nurses tend to pay attention to detail when interpreting fetal monitor tracings, while most doctors take a more general overview of the tracing. Ultimately, understanding how to interpret and discuss the baby's heart rate with your delivery team is important and will ensure everyone is on the same page.

Another key takeaway is that when you arrive at the hospital, it is important to take a look at your baby's heart rate on the fetal monitor. Understanding your baby's heart rate at the beginning of labor can provide a baseline for comparison later on. Throughout labor, you should keep a close eye on your baby's heart rate and be on the lookout for any concerning changes. If you have any questions or concerns about what you are seeing on the fetal monitor, get your delivery team involved.

Responding to Fetal Heart Rate Concerns

If your baby's heart rate is concerning, your delivery team may attempt simple interventions such as changing your position, starting intravenous fluids, or reducing Pitocin (if you are being induced) to improve the heart rate. However, if these interventions do not help, more advanced measures may be needed, like a C-section or operative vaginal birth if you are near the end of labor. The approach taken by your delivery team will depend on the specifics of your labor and your baby's condition. The most important thing is that your delivery team is actively monitoring your baby's heart rate and responding promptly to any concerning changes.

A more detailed explanation of these interventions is found in Chapter 10.

Assessing Contractions

Assessing the strength and frequency of your contractions during labor is just as crucial as monitoring your baby's heart rate. Both are interrelated and must be evaluated simultaneously. If there are any concerns about your baby's heart rate on the fetal monitor, it is critical to watch how they respond to contractions. As a natural part of labor, contractions place stress on the baby. If your baby is unable to handle the stress from contractions, their struggle will be reflected in their heart rate.

When assessing contractions, the first factor to consider is the frequency. A normal range is up to five contractions within a ten-minute period. Any more than that could be an indication that you are contracting too much. However, it is crucial to differentiate between natural contractions and those induced by Pitocin. If you are naturally contracting more than five times in a ten-minute window and the baby is fine, it may not be a big deal. However, if you are having more than five contractions in a ten-minute window while on Pitocin, it may mean that your Pitocin needs to be adjusted or turned down, particularly if the baby is starting to struggle.

The strength and duration of contractions become increasingly important as you approach delivery. If you are naturally experiencing strong and long contractions, it may be normal for you as long as the baby is handling them well. However, when contractions become strong and long due to Pitocin, it could take on a new meaning, particularly if it negatively affects your baby's heart rate.

When looking at your contractions, the type of fetal monitor used to graph your contractions will make a big difference on how they appear on the graph. An internal monitor measures the pressure inside your uterus, resulting in hill-like contractions on the graph. This is the most accurate way to assess your contractions. An external monitor cannot measure the pressure inside your uterus, but can tell if you are having contractions, resulting in jagged mountain-like lines on the graph.

In terms of assessing your contractions, there are two examples below. In the first example, a baby is doing well during contractions and is being monitored with an internal monitor. In the second example, the baby is not doing well during contractions. The fetal monitor in this example is external, so you can see the difference between how the contractions graph when an internal versus external monitor is used during labor.

MODERATE VARIABILITY DURING CONTRACTIONS
BABY IS HANDLING THE STRESS OF THE CONTRACTIONS

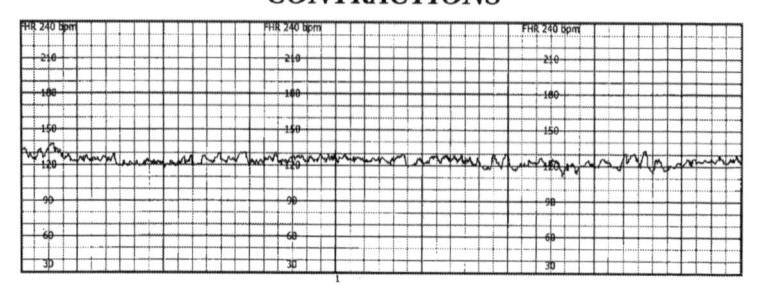

CONTRACTIONS INTERNAL MONITOR

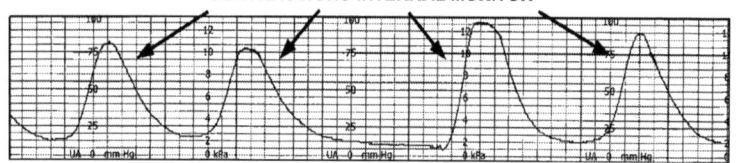

LATE DECELERATIONS WITH ABSENT TO MINIAL VARIABILITY
BABY IS UNDER TOO MUCH STRESS DURING CONTRACTIONS

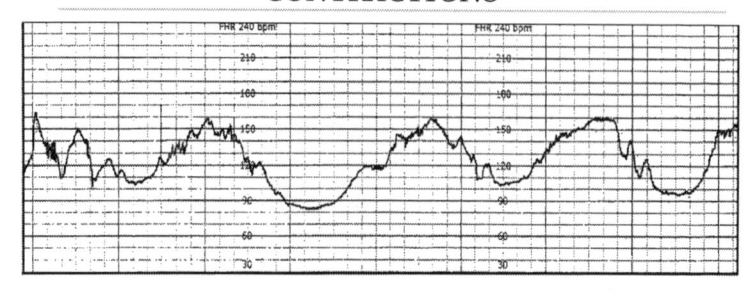

CONTRACTIONS EXTERNAL MONITOR

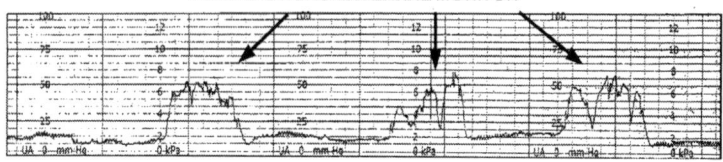

If you need help understanding how to read your contractions, do not hesitate to ask your nurse or someone from your delivery team. They can help you assess your contractions and compare them to your baby's heart rate. After reading this chapter, you now have a better understanding of the fetal monitor and the contractions, so you will be able to follow more easily what your nurse is saying.

Chapter 10

Tests to Evaluate Baby's Well-Being and Interventions during Labor

In many legal cases, when there is a concern about the baby, tests are performed to assess the baby and interventions are done to try to improve the baby's condition. Once a concern is identified, these are the first steps taken by the delivery team. Depending on which tests or interventions are carried out, the results are used to determine whether any changes need to be made to your labor plan

In situations where there are concerns about your baby's health, these tests and interventions become especially critical. This chapter helps you become familiar with them and provides guidance on the various issues that arise in legal baby cases concerning these interventions. Most importantly, delivery teams can get into trouble when they become falsely assured that baby is okay, or they take too long to assess the condition of the baby, resulting in a delayed delivery. This chapter provides essential information that every parent should know before going to the hospital, so they can make good decisions if these tests or interventions are done before or during labor.

Testing: Determine How the Baby Is Doing

Nonstress Test (NST)

A nonstress test involves monitoring the baby's heart rate for 20 minutes. The medical team will look for two accelerations in the baby's heart rate during this period. This is when the baby's heart rate speeds up for at least 15 seconds. When two accelerations occur, it is known as a reactive NST. However, if there are no accelerations, it is considered a non-reactive NST, indicating that the baby is not responding or moving as expected.

Biophysical Profile (BPP)

If your doctor is concerned about your baby's heart rate or if you had a nonreactive NST, they may perform a biophysical profile to assess your baby's overall health. During this procedure, an ultrasound machine is used in conjunction with a fetal monitor to evaluate various aspects of your baby's well-being, including their heart rate, breathing, body movement, muscle tone, and the amount of amniotic fluid. Each of these factors is given a score of 2, for a total possible score of 10. If your baby's score is 8 or less, your doctor may consider retesting or discussing other options with you if there are concerns about your baby's health.

Scalp Stimulation

In situations where there are concerns about your baby's heart rate while reviewing the fetal monitor tracing, your delivery team may try to stimulate your baby by scratching their scalp with their finger. This is done to see if the baby will move and create an acceleration on the fetal monitor tracing, which can be a reassuring sign. However, if the baby does not move, this can be a cause for concern, and your delivery team will discuss this with you during labor.

It is important to note that even if the baby does move in response to scalp stimulation, this may not always indicate that everything is okay. For example, in a legal case where a doctor performed a scalp stimulation on a baby who was showing signs of distress, the baby moved, and the doctor falsely assumed that everything was okay. As the doctor was reassured, the fetal monitor was removed for a short period; during this time, the baby was in serious trouble, but no one knew.

The lesson from this case is straightforward. It is critical that the fetal monitor stays on regardless of the results of a scalp stimulation so that your delivery team can continue to assess your baby's heart rate and ensure that there are no concerning changes. Remember the need for a scalp stimulation indicates that there are concerns about your baby's health, so it is important to closely watch their heart rate if the doctor performs a scalp stimulation, regardless of the result.

Vibroacoustic Stimulation "Buzz the Baby"

Vibroacoustic stimulation is a simple technique used to check on baby. It involves a device that emits a small amount of vibration and sound stimulation to the mother's abdomen, which can startle the baby so they wake up and move. The stimulation is usually applied for a short time, generally a few seconds. This method can be used at your doctor's office or in labor.

If the doctor uses the device to buzz your baby, there may be a concern about your baby's well-being, and it is essential to discuss with your doctor the possibility of starting the fetal monitor to check your baby's heart rate. This will help determine whether your baby is in a good or bad spot and allow your doctor to take appropriate action if needed.

Contraction Stress Test

A contraction stress test is done by looking at a fetal monitor and seeing how your baby is responding to the contractions. As you know, contractions can stress a baby, and this is completely normal. However, if something is up with the baby, they may not be able to handle the contractions. You can see this by watching your baby's heart rate as you have a contraction. If your baby's heart rate goes down when you have contractions, it may mean they are not doing well.

A contraction stress test can be a useful tool both during pregnancy and labor. In pregnancy, it is typically done with the help of a doctor or nurse, who will monitor the baby's heart rate during contractions. If you are not contracting, they can start Pitocin until you have three contractions in a ten-minute window.

In labor, you do not need a doctor or nurse to do a contraction stress test if you are already contracting. You or your baby advocate can look at the fetal monitor while you are having a contraction and see how your baby's heart rate responds. If your baby's heart rate goes down during a contraction and has a hard time recovering, it may indicate that your baby is experiencing too much stress during labor. If your baby's heart rate remains normal during a contraction, you know your baby is doing well. To complete the test, remember that you should have three contractions in 10 minutes.

Start an Internal Monitor

As mentioned in Chapter 8, an internal monitor is considered the gold standard for assessing a baby's heart rate and contraction pattern. This is because it provides precise and reliable data, allowing your healthcare provider to accurately assess your baby's well-being. If your healthcare provider is concerned about your baby's heart rate, they may recommend placing an internal monitor.

While some patients may be hesitant or uncomfortable with this type of monitoring, it is the most effective way to assess your baby's heart rate and ensure their safety.

Ultrasound

If the fetal monitor is having a difficult time picking up your baby's heart rate, the delivery team may use an ultrasound machine to check your baby's heart rate. This will typically happen if an external or wireless fetal monitor loses the baby's heart rate. In most cases, an internal monitor would wipe out the need for an ultrasound, but in legal baby cases, sometimes there is difficulty placing an internal monitor when a baby is in trouble, so they will use an ultrasound to check the baby's heart rate.

Interventions to Help the Baby

Intrauterine Resuscitative Measures

Intrauterine resuscitative measures are interventions that can be taken if your baby's heart rate becomes concerning during labor, which can indicate that the baby is not getting enough oxygen. While the name of the intervention may sound scary, it is simply a way for the delivery team to address any issues with the baby's oxygenation and ensure they can handle the stresses of labor. There are several things your nurse may do to help your baby:

- Change your position: Your nurse may turn you to your other side or put you on your hands and knees. This can help move the baby in case they are lying on their umbilical cord or the cord is compressed for some reason.
- Give you fluids by IV: This can help increase your blood volume and ensure better circulation to the baby.

- Start you on oxygen: Some hospitals may start oxygen through tubes in your nose, while others do not do this.

Your nurse will typically contact your doctor to inform them when any of these intrauterine resuscitative measures have been performed. However, there have been legal baby cases where the nurses do not contact the mom's doctor. It could be the middle of the night, or the baby's heart rate improved. However, in legal baby cases, nurses are criticized if they do not contact the mom's private doctor after this intervention.

If your nurse performs any of these interventions in response to your baby's heart rate, it is important to ask them if they have informed your doctor. This is a significant intervention that is intended to improve your baby's oxygen supply, so your doctor needs to be aware that it was done. This intervention may impact your doctor's recommendations for your care later in labor, so it is essential that they know when it was performed. Once your doctor has been informed, they can remotely evaluate your baby's heart rate and make any necessary adjustments to your labor plan if needed.

Amnioinfusion

Amnioinfusion is a procedure where fluid is infused into the uterus. It is performed to mimic the purpose of amniotic fluid, which acts as a cushion for your baby and the umbilical cord. IIf there is no amniotic fluid, the umbilical cord can become compressed, leading to a drop in the baby's heart rate in the form of variable decelerations. To address this, an amnioinfusion may be performed to increase the fluid in the uterus, which can relieve the pressure on the umbilical cord and reduce variable decelerations.

If variable decelerations occur during your labor, it is important to remain calm, as your delivery team will work to identify and fix the underlying issue. It is worth noting that the fact your team is performing an amnioinfusion indicates that they are engaged in your labor and monitoring your baby's health. If the decelerations persist despite the intervention, your team will discuss your options with you.

Turn Down or Shut Off Pitocin

If you are being induced with Pitocin and your baby's heart rate becomes concerning or you are having too many contractions, your nurse will likely turn down or shut off the Pitocin to address the issue. The reason for this is that too many contractions can reduce blood flow and oxygen to your baby, leading to too much stress. By decreasing the Pitocin, you enable the uterus to relax, allowing for improved blood flow and oxygen to reach your baby. This can give your baby the time needed to recover and prevent any further stress.

If the Pitocin is turned down or shut off, it is important to remember that this is a normal part of the induction process and does not necessarily mean that something is wrong. It may take longer for your labor to progress, as you may experience fewer or less intense contractions, but this can be very normal in labor.

Start a Tocolytic (Terbutaline)

If your contractions are too close together, your delivery team can give you terbutaline to slow down your contractions. Terbutaline works by relaxing the muscles in the uterus, giving your baby time to recover as it reduces the frequency of contractions.

Interventions During Vaginal Birth

Episiotomy

Episiotomy, a surgical cut made to the perineum, the region between the vaginal opening and the rectum, has traditionally been performed to widen the birth canal and aid in the delivery of the baby. However, its usage has been increasingly discouraged within the medical community due to its potential risks and limited benefits in most cases. Instead, alternative techniques like perineal massage and warm compresses are often preferred to prevent tearing during childbirth.

While the practice of episiotomy is generally discouraged, there are specific situations where your doctor may still recommend it. These include:

- High risk of severe laceration: If you are identified as being at a high risk of experiencing a third- or fourth-degree tear, which involves a tear extending into the muscle and anal sphincter.
- Concerning fetal heart rate: In cases where your baby's heart rate becomes worrisome,

necessitating a prompt delivery to mitigate potential complications.
- Shoulder dystocia: When the baby's shoulder becomes lodged behind the mother's pubic bone during delivery, requiring immediate intervention to ensure a safe birth.
- Expedited delivery: In certain circumstances, such as with a forceps delivery, where a faster delivery is deemed necessary for specific reasons.

Before labor and delivery, it is crucial to engage in an open discussion with your doctor regarding the potential risks and benefits of episiotomy. This dialogue will enable you to make informed decisions that are best for you and baby during your labor.

Assisted Vaginal Birth – Vacuum and Forceps

In certain situations, your doctor may opt to use forceps or a vacuum to assist in delivering your baby. These devices are applied to the baby's head, typically during a contraction while you are actively pushing. By applying controlled traction, your doctor can help facilitate the delivery process.

The use of forceps or vacuum may be considered when:
- Maternal exhaustion: If the mother is fatigued and unable to continue pushing effectively, these instruments can provide the necessary assistance to safely deliver the baby.
- Baby has a concerning heart rate: In cases where the baby's heart rate is abnormal and prompt

delivery is essential to avoid further complications, forceps or vacuum extraction may be utilized.

It is worth noting that while a vacuum extraction generally results in less vaginal trauma compared to forceps, forceps have a higher success rate in delivering babies.

Chapter 11

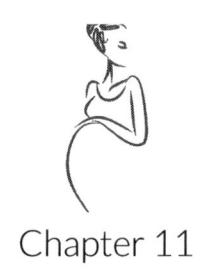

Learning from the Legal Baby Cases to Avoid Future Mistakes

Through a two-decade analysis of legal baby cases, it became apparent that there were reoccurring issues, facts, and timeframes present in many cases. Drawing on this knowledge, I have identified the 10 most common factors in legal baby cases that every parent should be aware of as they prepare for childbirth. By being informed and aware of these, you can approach labor and delivery with a heightened sense of awareness. This awareness, combined with the tips in this chapter for your labor and delivery, will help you make informed decisions to avoid similar complications during your labor and delivery.

#1 Pitocin

When a new case comes in, the most common words I read are "mom is being induced with Pitocin." Pitocin is the most common fact in a legal baby case. When Pitocin is an issue in a case, it is because it caused too many contractions. This can result in the baby not getting enough oxygen during labor and delivery. Likewise, although uncommon, it can cause the uterus to tear open, which is called a uterine rupture. This is an obstetrical emergency that affects both mom and baby.

It is important to understand a crucial distinction when it comes to Pitocin in legal baby cases. While Pitocin is almost always used in the labors, it is not always the primary issue in the case. In fact, Pitocin usage flies under the radar in some cases. For example, in cases of shoulder dystocia, where a baby's shoulder gets stuck in the birth canal, Pitocin is a common factor. However, in such cases, the focus of the legal claim is typically on whether the physicians handled the delivery of the baby's shoulder properly, rather than on the management of Pitocin. So while the use of Pitocin may be a contributing factor, it may not necessarily be the main point of contention in the legal baby case. It is important to understand that while Pitocin can be administered correctly, it can still lead to complications during labor.

Tips for Your Labor and Delivery

When it comes to Pitocin, it is crucial to understand that the drug causes the uterus to contract in a way that may differ from natural contractions. Your natural contractions may not have been as strong or frequent. One study found that

Pitocin in labor changes a mother's contraction pattern.[1] The impact of unnatural contractions is unique to each patient and the ripple effect of how your body responds is relatively unknown until you are in labor.

As you will not know how your body responds to Pitocin, it would be prudent to start with a low dose, with minimal increases that are spaced out. This will help you hit your "sweet spot," which is the optimal amount of Pitocin you need to deliver your baby without your body contracting too much. Some doctors and delivery teams already take this approach. This is not new information that is going to rock the Pitocin world. The problem is that while some doctors follow this protocol, others do not.

There is much debate among doctors regarding the use of Pitocin during labor and delivery. In one legal case, I had a doctor explain to me that the delivery team blew a hole in the mom's uterus with too much Pitocin. Another doctor looked at the same care and was personally insulted by such an opinion. Similarly, one doctor will tell me that the Pitocin should not have been increased as mom's contractions were adequate, while another doctor will tell me it was okay to increase the Pitocin as the contractions were not adequate. In fact, it seems that doctors disagree on nearly every aspect

---

1 Olsson et al., "Maternal and newborn plasma oxytocin levels in response to maternal synthetic oxytocin administration during labour, birth and postpartum – a systematic review with implications for the function of the oxytocinergic," BMC Pregnancy Childbirth 23 (2023): 137.

of Pitocin, with one notable exception: it is generally considered safe to use during labor and delivery.

If you are considering a Pitocin induction, it is crucial to have a candid conversation with your doctor about their approach and to make sure it aligns with your preferences. If you prefer a more gradual induction process, be sure to communicate this to your doctor beforehand and confirm that they are willing to accommodate your wishes. Pitocin inductions vary from doctor to doctor, so having this discussion with your physician before going into labor is critical.

In addition, when considering a Pitocin induction, it can be helpful to gather advice and insights from other moms who have gone through the process. Reach out to other moms and ask them about their experience with Pitocin. You might ask if there is anything they would have done differently and if they have any advice for you. In my experience, talking to other moms can be especially helpful, as they can provide unique insights and firsthand accounts. In fact, many moms who have had difficult childbirth experiences involving a "close call" or other complications report having received Pitocin during labor. By seeking the perspectives of other moms, you can get a better sense of what to expect and what questions to ask your doctor before your induction.

Overall, if you are considering a Pitocin induction, it is essential to understand how to make it as safe as possible. To assist you, I have compiled a list of 14 tips to consider, based on legal cases involving Pitocin. These tips are designed to provide you with a solid starting point for a safe Pitocin induction. *(see Chapter 14)*

#2 Water Breaking

In the majority of legal cases related to childbirth, complications tend to arise after the mother's water breaks. These issues can occur either immediately after the amniotic sac ruptures, as has been documented in some cases, or they may manifest themselves hours or even days later. It is noteworthy that such difficulties can arise whether the doctor manually breaks the amniotic sac or if it happens naturally. The critical point to note is that infants often face challenges once the amniotic fluid has drained out.

Tips for Your Labor and Delivery

When your water breaks, it signifies the onset of labor. This triggers the body to start contracting and should also serve as a signal to monitor the baby's heart rate closely. If you plan to use an external or wireless monitor during labor, it is crucial to ensure that it continues to graph the baby's heart rate accurately for at least 30 minutes after the water breaks. In cases where the baby encountered complications soon after the water broke, both the external and wireless monitors struggled to track the baby's heart rate, causing a delay in delivery while doctors tried to identify the issue. Of note, an internal monitor placed right after your water breaks would help avoid the spotty monitoring often associated with an external or wireless monitor.

If your doctor recommends breaking your bag of water, it is crucial to understand why they suggest it. It is essential to note that there is a lower chance of complications during labor before the water breaks, making this a significant decision. Therefore, weighing the benefits and risks carefully before agreeing to this recommendation is important.

#3 Umbilical Cord

In many legal cases, the umbilical cord is wrapped around some part of the baby during delivery. The cord may be wrapped around the baby's shoulder, arm, neck, or legs and is typically noted to be tightly wound. Although we cannot see what happens in the uterus as the baby descends into the birth canal, some experts have suggested that the descent can tighten the umbilical cord, leading to compression and decreased oxygen supply to the baby.

Tips for Your Labor and Delivery

The lesson to be learned is that continuous monitoring of the baby's heart rate will help identify cord problems. The delivery team is likely unaware that the baby is tangled in the cord before birth. However, when the cord is compressed from being tangled around the baby, it reduces blood flow and oxygen, resulting in a drop in the baby's heart rate, which is usually seen as variable decelerations. As long as the baby's heart rate is being monitored, these changes can be identified, and the delivery team can intervene to relieve the pressure on the cord. If this occurs toward the end of labor, your doctor may use a vacuum or forceps to expedite the baby's descent and delivery.

#4 Meconium

A common factor in legal baby cases is the presence of meconium, which refers to the baby's first bowel movement. Meconium can vary in consistency from light to thick and can be detected before delivery if the baby has passed it before your water breaks. If this happens, your amniotic fluid will be a greenish-brown color. However, meconium can also be passed after your bag of water breaks, and this may only be discovered after delivery.

It is important to note that meconium aspiration is a significant concern when meconium is present in the amniotic fluid. Meconium aspiration occurs when the baby inhales or aspirates the meconium into their lungs. This can lead to various respiratory problems, such as lung inflammation and potentially severe breathing difficulties.

Tips for Your Labor and Delivery

If your baby has passed meconium, the recommendations by your doctor and the delivery team will be based on your entire clinical picture. Whether the recommendation is a C-section or another plan will likely depend on your doctor and could depend on which hospital you are at. A small hospital will not have the specialized care your baby will need if they have meconium in their lungs. Hence, they may make a different recommendation than if you were at a big hospital with specialized care.

While passing meconium before birth can be normal, it can also mean that the baby has undergone some stress before your water broke. The reason a baby passed meconium can be difficult to determine, as there is no way to assess the environment in the uterus. If your baby's fluid is stained with meconium, you need to be asking questions to help you make a good, informed decision about how you plan on delivering your baby. These questions should be at the top of your mind:

- Talk to your doctor about the risk of meconium aspiration as it applies to your specific situation.
- Talk to your doctor about their thoughts on having a C-section to get the baby out of the environment.
- Ask about the specific risks to the baby of a vaginal delivery versus a C-section when meconium is present.
- Ask your doctor whether there is anything that indicates your baby passed meconium due to stress.
- Are there other factors like low amniotic fluid that you should be concerned about?
- Ask to speak with the pediatrician or the neonatologist at the hospital and get their thoughts on meconium and how this will impact your baby at birth.
- Ask your doctor, if this was your pregnancy (or your wife's pregnancy), what would you do?

Other things to consider are talking to your doctor about placing an internal fetal monitor for the most accurate method to watch your baby's heart rate. Also, ensure your baby advocate closely watches you and your baby during labor.

Overall, the biggest lesson to learn is that meconium can negatively affect your baby, so asking questions and making an informed decision is very important when meconium is present.

#5 Wrong Type of Fetal Monitor

A common issue in a baby case is that the wrong type of fetal monitoring was being used to monitor the baby's heart rate and contractions. This comes into play when they use an external or wireless monitor, and the baby's heart rate starts to have concerning changes. The main sign of potential problems is that the baby's heart rate slows down or decelerates, or the variability of the heart rate decreases. When this happens, many doctors believe an internal monitor should be placed to better assess the heart rate and contractions. If the delivery team does not switch out the fetal monitors when there are concerns about the baby, they can get criticized in legal baby cases if there is a bad outcome.

Tips for Your Labor and Delivery

If the delivery team expresses concern about your baby's heart rate, it is important that they offer you the option of monitoring your baby with an internal monitor. However, in legal baby cases, many delivery teams fail to provide this option. If you are unsure whether the delivery team should offer you the option of an internal monitor, a good rule of thumb is to ask them about it when they are performing any of the interventions discussed in Chapter 10. If an intervention is performed that suggests the delivery team is concerned about your baby's condition, they should offer you the option of an internal monitor to help identify any potential issues. Failing to do so could result in legal problems if something goes wrong that could have been detected with an internal monitor.

#6 Lack of Intervention

In many legal baby cases, the delivery team is faulted for not intervening during labor and delivery. This means that moms were not given all their options, or if they were, it was not given to mom in time. It is essential to understand that in most cases, the mistake made by the delivery team is due to something not being done or not offered to the mom.

Tips for Your Labor and Delivery

During labor and delivery, it is crucial to prioritize effective communication. By actively engaging with your delivery team, asking pertinent questions, and taking a proactive approach, you can minimize the risk of miscommunication, which often leads to inadequate interventions. Equipping yourself with knowledge about labor and delivery empowers you to ask the right questions and gather valuable information from your delivery team. This, in turn, ensures that you receive comprehensive guidance and are presented with all available options throughout the process.

When examining past legal cases involving babies, a significant observation emerges: none of the families involved in the legal cases were healthcare professionals that had experience delivering babies. This implies that individuals with a solid understanding of labor and delivery, including the interpretation of the baby's heart rate, as well as various interventions and available options, are less likely to be involved in legal baby cases. Their knowledge of labor and delivery enables them to navigate the process more effectively, thereby avoiding the mistakes and challenges faced by other families.

#7 Residents

When it comes to residents in a legal baby case, they always ask the same question. "Do I testify as to what I would have known as a resident, or do I testify as to what I know now, years later?" It is a valid question in a legal proceeding, but a little concerning when this is the person talking to and updating your doctor on the status of your labor.

A common issue in legal baby cases is that the resident did not correctly describe the baby's heart rate to the doctor or did not make timely contact with the doctor when the baby's heart rate became concerning. It is very common for a physician to be upset with residents in legal baby cases. This is because most of the time, the doctor would have delivered the baby earlier had they known what was happening with the baby's heart rate.

Tips for Your Labor and Delivery

The medical world is fully aware that moms need a second set of eyes on them and the baby during labor, and thus designate the nurse as the advocate for the mom and her baby. The nurse's role as advocate takes on a completely different meaning when residents are involved in labor and delivery. If the residents are short-circuiting and making bad recommendations, your nurse must step in and protect you and your baby. They do this by talking to the doctor directly or getting help from their charge nurse.

Through conversations with nurses, it became clear that residents fall into one of three categories: great doctors, arrogant know-it-alls, or somewhere in the middle. Nurses are typically familiar with the residents' personalities and level of expertise, enabling them to make informed judgments on when to advocate for the mother and her baby.

However, it is worth noting that if you have a timid or inexperienced nurse, they may not feel confident challenging questionable decisions or recommendations made by residents. In fact, many legal cases involving babies often involve inexperienced nurses. When assessing a nurse's involvement in a legal case, the first question I always ask is, "How long have you been a labor and delivery nurse?" Similarly, it would be beneficial for you to ask your nurse this question, as it can provide insight into how they might respond to poor decisions made by residents.

If you find yourself with an inexperienced nurse and have concerns about the care you are receiving from the residents, request to speak to the charge nurse. The charge nurse oversees all the nurses and can assist you in addressing any concerns you may have about your care or the residents. It is important to note that charge nurses are typically experienced, which is why they are in charge and hold a leadership position.

If you anticipate the involvement of residents in your labor and delivery, it is crucial to discuss this with your doctor during your pregnancy. In certain hospitals, residents are responsible for managing the labor and delivery unit as part of their training to become doctors. They may play a significant role on your special day, so it is vital to understand this dynamic and be prepared accordingly.

#8 Busy Labor and Delivery Units

If you arrive at the hospital and find a full house on the labor and delivery unit, it is important to keep in mind that your delivery team may be busy. This could lead to a problem if you or your baby require immediate attention. If your doctor is not at the hospital, you will have to rely on the in-house hospital doctor, who may also be occupied with another patient. Your nurse will be busy attending to other patients, which could be problematic if your baby requires their undivided attention.

In one legal case, a mom arrived at the hospital to deliver her baby and the labor and delivery floor at the hospital was very busy. Upon starting the external fetal monitor, it was discovered that the baby's heart rate was concerning, prompting the nurse to call in the in-house hospital doctor. The very busy doctor quickly assessed the mom and her baby and was assured that everything was fine with the baby, and then left the room. The nurse informed the patient's private doctor about the concerning heart rate, and the doctor stated that they were on their way to the hospital, but it was rush hour, so it would take some time to get there. While waiting for the private doctor to arrive, the external fetal monitor was having difficulty graphing the baby's heart rate, but no one attempted to fix it due to the unit being overwhelmed with patients. As time passed, the nurse returned to the patient's room and tried to adjust the monitor but could not locate the baby's heart rate. Eventually, the in-house doctor returned and requested an ultrasound machine, which confirmed that the baby had no heartbeat, leading to the tragic news that the baby had passed away while the mom waited for her private doctor to arrive at the hospital.

In this case, the delivery team was spread thin and running hard that day. However, it is worth considering what might have happened if the same patient had arrived on a normal or slow day. It is possible that the concerning heart rate of the baby would have been handled differently, and the outcome better.

Tips for Your Labor and Delivery

No one knows how busy a labor and delivery unit will be on a particular day. If you go into labor on a busy day and have concerns about your baby, speak up immediately. There may be some lag time between your request to see a doctor and when they can attend to you. The delivery team will prioritize patients, so if you speak up and they end up placing an internal monitor that shows your baby is in trouble, they will get to you faster than someone who has stalled out in labor, and their baby is fine. In the case example, if the team had placed an internal monitor when the mom arrived at the hospital, it would have shown that the baby was deteriorating while waiting for her private doctor to get to the hospital. The delivery team would have known something was wrong and could have responded appropriately.

If there are any concerns whatsoever about your baby, it is important that there is continuous monitoring of their heart rate. For example, if the hospital performs tests to check your baby's well-being, like scalp stimulation, it is crucial to make sure your baby's heart rate continues to graph after the test is performed to identify any negative changes. In the case mentioned earlier, if the family knew how important it was to make sure the baby's heart rate was graphing on the fetal monitor, it may have changed the outcome. They could have alerted the nurse immediately that the baby's heart rate was not graphing continuously, prompting the nurse to act quickly and get the baby's heart rate back on the monitor. When a nurse is running hard, these important details can get overlooked, making it important for families to have the knowledge of labor and delivery and to be proactive to protect their baby.

#9 Shift Changes

Shift change is a busy time on the labor and delivery unit, as one team concludes their work and another team takes over. Typically, the labor and delivery unit operates on a 12-hour work schedule, with teams working 12-hour shifts. Shift change commonly occurs around 7:00 a.m. and 7:00 p.m., during which the incoming delivery team receives report from the outgoing team about each patient on the floor.

Shift change is a vulnerable time when errors can occur. It is noteworthy that the morning shift change at 7:00 a.m. is particularly common in legal baby cases. This transition marks the departure of the night team and the commencement of the morning team. As the night shift nears its end, team members may exhibit certain tendencies, such as taking specific actions or refraining from doing so, knowing that their shift is about to conclude. Simultaneously, the incoming delivery team begins their rounds and checking on the patients. With a fresh set of eyes now focused on the laboring mothers, different recommendations may be made, or concerns may arise that were not addressed by the previous team.

Tips for Your Labor and Delivery

Recognizing the potential for mistakes during shift changes is crucial. Specifically, between 6:00 a.m. and 8:00 a.m., it is essential for you and your baby advocate to maintain a heightened sense of awareness. It is strongly advised that your advocate remains by your side during this period, despite the possibility of wanting to take a break due to the duration of your labor.

During this transition, you say goodbye to one delivery team while being introduced to the new team responsible for your care. It is vital to carefully observe any indications of concern that the new team may have regarding the well-being of your baby. Pay attention to any interventions they initiate, such as recommending the use of an internal fetal monitor to closely watch your baby's heart rate, or if they contact your private doctor and request they come to the hospital. In many legal baby cases, the fresh perspective of the new team often leads to changes. Their arrival can bring about adjustments in the approach to your care or discoveries that were overlooked by the previous team.

#10 Delayed Delivery - The Baby's Heart Rate on the Fetal Monitor

In legal baby cases, the first 9 common issues or facts in this chapter all boil down to one crucial common factor: the baby's heart rate on the fetal monitor. Whether the baby experiences complications due to Pitocin use, if there are problems arising from the mother's water breaking, the wrong type of fetal monitor was being used, or if there are errors due to a busy labor and delivery unit, the ultimate outcome rests on the baby's heart rate and what could have been done differently for a healthy baby.

In legal cases, the delivery of the baby is usually done by an emergency C-section or an operative vaginal delivery, which involves using forceps or a vacuum to expedite delivery. The most common problem is when the delivery team fails to offer the mom the option of a C-section or operative vaginal delivery earlier in labor, causing a delay in the delivery of the baby that leads to a permanent injury.

In these cases, timing is critical and the window of opportunity for intervention is short. An injury to the infant typically occurs 20 minutes before birth, although this may vary. It is important to recognize that a baby's health can deteriorate quickly during this time, underscoring the importance of prompt action by the delivery team.

Tips for Your Labor and Delivery

The key lesson parents can learn from the delay in delivery, is that early intervention by the delivery team in response to a concerning heart rate on the fetal monitor is crucial. There is a process that delivery teams follow to determine whether delivery needs to be expedited or whether labor should continue. This process takes time as the team tries to determine what is wrong inside the uterus that is affecting the baby. Since they cannot see the baby directly, they must rely on testing, interventions, and their overall assessment of the baby. A quick overview of this process usually involves the following:

1. Step #1 Concerning heart rate of the baby, usually with decelerations, possibly decreased variability or bradycardia.
2. Step #2 Delivery team tries to improve or fix the heart rate through interventions like turning mom

to her side, giving fluids, stopping Pitocin, etc. (*See Chapter 10 for types of interventions.*)
3. Step #3 We have tried everything and cannot fix the baby's heart rate. Recommend C-section or operative vaginal delivery.

The earlier the delivery team responds to a concern about your baby, the sooner they can start the process of determining how your baby is doing and whether they need to speed up delivery.

In situations where there is a delay getting to the mother, it is common that it was due to a busy day on the labor and delivery floor. When I meet with the delivery team regarding a baby case, they frequently mention how busy the unit was that day. To address this, having a baby advocate by your bedside with the primary responsibility of monitoring your baby and watching for any concerning changes in their heart rate can be helpful. This can be particularly important on a busy day, as they can promptly notify the delivery team if necessary.

Another crucial lesson to learn is the distinction between forceps and a vacuum during an operative vaginal delivery. Forceps are a more reliable method to deliver the baby than a vacuum. If a vacuum pops off three times or after three pulls, the delivery team will convert to a C-section, which consumes a lot of time when the baby is in trouble. Experts have explained that forceps do not "pop off," so using them in the first place may result in faster delivery. Otherwise, you run the risk of the vacuum not working, plus the time it takes to perform a C-section. When this happens, it has delayed deliveries in legal baby cases when every second counted. Remember, it is usually in the final 20 minutes of the labor that the baby will sustain an irreversible injury, so using the fastest method to get your baby delivered is important.

If you experience the mad dash to the operating room or the chaos that engulfs labor and delivery when a delivery team is racing against the clock to deliver a healthy baby, try your best to stay calm. Understand that your delivery team is trained to respond to emergency situations by moving fast, getting additional help, and using interventions to get your baby safely delivered. While this may seem like a cause for concern, it is important to remember that this is also the path to a healthy baby.

Chapter 12
Are Epidurals Safe in Labor?

Epidurals can be one of the more intimidating aspects of labor for some women. You will be asked to sit up and hunch over while a needle is inserted into your back during the procedure. Although the process may be uncomfortable and nerve-wracking, the good news is that it is typically a quick procedure that can provide immediate relief from contractions.

If you are considering getting an epidural, this chapter is a must-read. It provides essential information on the safe administration of epidurals, potential risks involved, and important points to keep in mind before arriving to the hospital.

Epidural Procedure and Monitoring

Before receiving an epidural, the anesthesiologist will conduct a thorough pre-anesthesia evaluation. This includes asking about your medical history, performing a physical examination to assess your airway, vital signs, heart, lungs, and back, and discussing the potential risks and benefits of the procedure with you. If you have any questions or concerns, this is the time to address them.

Once you have given your consent, the anesthesiologist will perform a "time-out" to verify your identity and confirm that the correct procedure is being performed. Then, you will be asked to sit up on the edge of the bed while the epidural is administered. The anesthesiologist will closely monitor your oxygen saturation, heart rate, and blood pressure throughout the procedure to ensure your safety.

After the epidural is in place, the anesthesiologist should remain with you for at least 15–20 minutes to ensure that everything is working properly and that you are feeling comfortable.

Do Not Practice on Me

When it comes to getting an epidural for pain relief during labor, it is important to know who will be administering the epidural. You want an experienced and board-certified anesthesiologist performing the epidural placement. While some residents or CRNAs place an epidural under the supervision of an anesthesiologist, it is best to have it done by the anesthesiologist who is in charge.

During the pre-anesthesia evaluation, be sure to ask who will be placing your epidural and confirm that it is an experienced anesthesiologist. Feeling comfortable and confident in the person administering your epidural is important.

Remember that an epidural is a medical procedure with potential risks, so it is crucial to have a skilled and experienced professional handling the placement.

Test Dose

When an epidural is placed, the anesthesiologist should perform a test dose to ensure that the epidural medication is not accidentally administered into your bloodstream, as the blood could carry the anesthesia to your heart. During the test dose, a small amount of medication is injected into the epidural space in your lower spine, and the anesthesiologist monitors your vital signs for changes. If your heart rate increases by 20 percent or more, it may indicate that the medication has entered your bloodstream, and the epidural placement needs to be adjusted. If the test dose has no effect on your vital signs, the anesthesiologist will proceed to administer the epidural medication. Not all doctors use the test dose method, so it is crucial to discuss this with the anesthesiologist before the procedure to ensure that all necessary safety measures are taken.

Intralipids

A crash cart is a cart on wheels that has lifesaving supplies and is used when a code is called, or someone needs to be resuscitated. There should be a crash cart on labor and delivery with intralipids. This medication will reverse the side effects of the anesthesia if it enters your bloodstream. The crash cart should be very close when you are getting an epidural. It is important to ask how fast the delivery team can get intralipids or where the crash cart is before your epidural procedure. If you ask where the crash cart is, the anesthesiologist may look at you like you are crazy because it is supposed to be standard to have intralipids close by when placing an epidural. "Of course, it is nearby," should be the response from the anesthesiologist, as they likely wonder why you are asking such a question.

Do not underestimate the importance of having intralipids close to you to reverse the anesthesia if it enters your bloodstream. If this medication is not near you, it can cause a delay that could be the difference between life and death.

Baby Advocate and the Epidural

When it comes to getting an epidural, it is crucial to be aware of hospital policies regarding who can be in the room during the procedure. Some hospitals may ask family members to leave during the procedure, but it is important that someone stays with you at all times.

As you learned in Chapter 1, a tragic case occurred when a mother passed away after receiving an epidural. It is important to know that her family was not present during the procedure. While the details of this tragedy cannot be disclosed, it serves as a stark reminder of the importance of having a baby advocate. Your baby advocate, or a family member, should remain by your side, especially during any procedure that carries a risk of death. Having someone there to advocate for you and monitor your condition can potentially save your life. It is also critical to follow the recommendations in this chapter to minimize the risks associated with getting an epidural.

Pro Tip

If you plan on getting an epidural or you are considering the possibility, talk to your doctor ahead of time. It is highly recommended that your baby advocate or family member stay close to you during this procedure to ensure you receive the proper care and attention.

Unplanned C-Section or Operative Delivery

If you have an epidural in place, you may be better prepared for a potential C-section. This can help avoid the need for general anesthesia during an unplanned C-section, as the anesthesiologist has already assessed your condition and can easily convert your labor anesthesia to anesthesia for the C-section. Having an epidural in place may be particularly beneficial for patients who have previously undergone a C-section, are carrying multiple babies, or if there are any concerns about the baby's heart rate during labor.

Do Epidurals Affect Labor Progress?

An epidural can affect the pushing stage or the second stage of labor, as the epidural can impact the muscles used to push the baby out. In some cases, the time spent in this stage may be extended due to the effect of the epidural. The density of the epidural can also impact your ability to push effectively. A dense epidural refers to a high concentration of anesthesia in the epidural space, which can result in a more complete block of sensation and muscle control. This can make it more challenging for you to feel the pressure and urge to push, which can ultimately prolong the second stage of labor. Additionally, a dense epidural may cause a decrease in muscle strength, making it more difficult for you to push your baby out effectively. Therefore, if the epidural is too dense, it may need to be adjusted to allow for better muscle control during delivery.

Pro Tip

In cases where there are concerns about your baby's heart rate, it may be advisable to consider skipping the epidural. This is because if your baby is experiencing too much stress in labor, it is important to get them out as quickly and effectively as possible. If you are unable to push effectively due to the effects of the epidural, your baby may be at risk of further stress, which could result in the need for interventions such as vacuum or forceps-assisted delivery, or even an emergency C-section. It is important to discuss with your doctor the risks and benefits of an epidural, particularly if there are any concerns about your baby's well-being during labor.

Pitocin Induction and Epidural

When it comes to legal baby cases, it is common for moms to receive an epidural during a Pitocin induction. Since most moms opt for an epidural during labor, this combination is not unusual. However, it is worth noting that when a mom undergoes a Pitocin induction, it means she is being given a synthetic hormone to stimulate the uterus and cause contractions. These contractions can often be stronger and more intense than natural contractions. When an epidural is administered, it can block the pain associated with these contractions, making it difficult to know if they are too strong.

Without the ability to feel your contractions, it is essential to closely monitor the contractions and the baby's heart rate for any signs of stress. This is where an internal monitor can be useful, as it provides the most accurate way to assess both.

It is also important to note that research has shown the combination of Pitocin and an epidural may increase the likelihood of an operative vaginal delivery, such as using a vacuum or forceps.[2] This is because epidurals can slow down labor and make it harder for women to push effectively, while Pitocin can increase the strength and frequency of contractions, similar to speeding up labor. This can further exhaust a mom, particularly if she has already been in labor for a prolonged period.

It is crucial to have a conversation with your doctor about the risks and benefits of both Pitocin and an epidural and how they may impact your labor and delivery. By discussing

---

2   Angeliki Antonakou and Dimitrios Papoutsis, "The Effect of Epidural Analgesia on the Delivery Outcome of Induced Labour: A Retrospective Case Series," *Obstetrics and Gynecology International* 2016 (2016): pp. 1-5, https://doi.org/10.1155/2016/5740534.

these options with your doctor, you can make an informed decision about what is best for you and your baby.

Epidurals and Autism

There is an ongoing debate and conflicting evidence regarding the potential link between epidurals and the risk of autism in babies. While some studies suggest a possible association, others have found no evidence of a causal relationship. In 2020, the American College of Obstetricians and Gynecologists (ACOG) released a joint statement with other organizations stating that epidurals are safe and do not cause autism.[3] However, keep in mind that there are different viewpoints and opinions on this issue, and your doctor may have their own perspective. Therefore, if you are interested in researching this topic further, it is worth discussing it with your doctor to get their insight.

---

3   American College of Obstetricians and Gynecologists, Society for Obstetric Anesthesia and Perinatology, American Society of Anesthesiologists, Society for Pediatric Anesthesia, and Society for Maternal-Fetal Medicine. "Labor Epidurals Do Not Cause Autism; Safe for Mothers and Infants: Joint Statement of the Society for Obstetric Anesthesia and Perinatology, American Society of Anesthesiologists, Society for Pediatric Anesthesia, American College of Obstetricians and Gynecologists, and the Society for Maternal-Fetal Medicine." Accessed October 13, 2020.

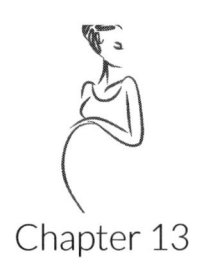

Chapter 13
Understanding the C-Section Option before and during Labor

In the world of legal childbirth cases, C-sections are a common procedure. Mothers may be given the option of a C-section during labor, and they may also be presented with the option of a C-section before labor or upon arrival at the hospital. If this is a decision that has to be made while you are at the hospital, it is often a time-sensitive one that requires quick thinking and informed decision-making. That is why it is important to have a general understanding of C-sections ahead of time so that you can be prepared to make the best decision for you and your baby.

Arriving at the Hospital: C-Section versus Vaginal Delivery

When you arrive at labor and delivery, your doctor may offer you the option of a C-section or vaginal delivery depending on your unique situation. This could include concerns about the health of the baby or you, a breech presentation, or other complications that may increase the risk to your baby during a vaginal delivery. If they are offering you the option of a C-section when you arrive to labor and delivery, then there is a concern of some sort or medical reason for doing so.

These discussions and decisions on whether to deliver your baby by C-section or natural birth should not be taken lightly. If you are approached with these two options when you arrive to the hospital, this can turn into a very important choice—perhaps one of the most important ones you will have to make concerning the birth of your baby. To demonstrate this point, consider the following three life stories.

In Sam's case *(see Introduction)*, my sister was concerned about the well-being of the baby when they arrived at the hospital, and she felt that a C-section was the best option. However, Sam had different thoughts and did not want a C-section; instead, she chose to deliver her baby naturally. She ultimately made a good choice and delivered a healthy baby girl. In contrast, in a legal baby case, the delivery team offered the mother the option of a C-section and vaginal delivery, and the soon-to-be grandma pushed for the C-section for the baby's safety. However, the mother refused the C-section against her mom's wishes and chose to deliver the baby naturally. Unfortunately, in that legal baby case, the grandmother was right that the C-section was the safer route for the baby. Experts in that case believed that if the mother had chosen the option of a C-section when she arrived at the hospital the baby would have been born healthy, instead of suffering permanent injury.

The story of Ali's delivery *(see Chapter 5)* is another example of the importance of the C-section decision. In her case, the doctor recommended a vaginal delivery, but her baby advocate was on the side of a C-section. Ultimately, Ali chose to have a C-section, and her baby was born safely. According to the doctor, this may not have been the case if Ali chose a vaginal delivery.

Since no one has a crystal ball that can predict the future, these discussions about whether to have a C-section or vaginal delivery are challenging. To help you make an informed decision if you are offered both options when you arrive to the hospital, consider the following:

1.) Is the labor and delivery unit busy? *(This means you may not be getting the attention you need during labor.)*
2.) Is the labor and delivery unit going to be understaffed for any reason during my labor? *(This could come into play at night.)*
3.) If I choose a vaginal delivery, what are the chances that I may end up with a C-section anyway?
4.) If I choose a vaginal delivery, will the surgeon and anesthesiologist remain at the hospital in case I need a C-section quickly?
5.) Do I like and trust my delivery team?
6.) If I choose a C-section, who will be performing it now, versus if I end up needing one later in labor?

7.) What are the risks to my baby and me if I deliver the baby naturally versus by C-section?

When considering the choice between a C-section and a vaginal delivery, it is crucial to understand your doctor's stance on the matter. Are they presenting both options as safe alternatives, or are they recommending one over the other? This distinction holds significant weight in your decision-making process. If your doctor believes that both methods can be carried out safely, then you have a significant decision to make.

It is important to note that if your doctor is offering you a C-section as an option, there is likely a concern regarding either your well-being or that of the baby. This consideration should be taken seriously when contemplating a vaginal delivery. Opting for a vaginal delivery under such circumstances may require additional attention and care from your delivery team compared to a mother who is not being presented with the option of a C-section due to medical reasons.

Another factor to consider is the environment and comfort level you have with your delivery team. If the labor and delivery unit is busy or if you feel uncomfortable with your delivery team, this should be factored into your decision-making process. Ultimately, ensuring your comfort, safety, and the well-being of both you and your baby should guide you in making a good decision.

Emergency C-Section

In the case of an emergency C-section, time is of the essence. This type of C-section may be recommended if there are any complications with the baby or mother and delivery must be expedited for the safety of either one.

Experts emphasize the 30-minute rule when it comes to emergency C-sections. This means from decision to incision, the maximum time it should take to perform the C-section is 30 minutes. However, there is some debate about whether this rule applies to all hospitals or only to smaller community hospitals. For instance, in a smaller community hospital, the 30-minute rule would come into play if the anesthesiologist was not at the hospital, but required to arrive within 20 minutes of being called for a C-section. This way, the delivery can still be done within the 30-minute rule.

In larger hospitals where all necessary staff are on hand, a C-section can be performed much faster than in a smaller community hospital. A common question in a deposition of a doctor from a larger hospital, is how fast a C-section can be accomplished in an emergency, and the answer is usually 10 minutes or less. Although there is a 30-minute rule, in a true emergency, the delivery team pays no attention to it and moves as quickly and safely as possible to deliver the baby.

As a patient, it is essential to remember that delivering at a larger hospital with everyone on-site will likely result in a faster delivery as compared to a smaller community hospital if you need an emergency C-section.

Elective C-Section

My sister informed me that her daughter was planning on delivering her baby vaginally because she believed that C-sections were too dangerous for babies. I was taken aback by this statement and immediately responded, "What are you smoking? That is not true." As a legal professional who specializes in cases involving babies, I have never seen or heard of a legal case involving an elective C-section that resulted in harm to the baby. In fact, in my field, an elective C-section at 39 weeks is considered the safest option for the baby.

Many baby lawyers choose an elective C-section because of the low risk of injury to the baby. I remember back in 2003, when elective C-sections were still controversial, I asked a friend who was an attorney how she was planning to deliver her baby. She looked at me with a straight face and said that her doctor would be performing a C-section even if she had to tell him she was "screaming with herpes." At that time, if a woman had vaginal herpes, the recommendation was to have a C-section, and my friend got her C-section.

A few years later, when elective C-sections became more acceptable, another friend who was an attorney wanted his wife to have an elective C-section at 39 weeks. However, he requested six doctors to be present in the operating room during the C-section. We never could figure out if he was joking about the number of doctors, but it was clear that even the thought of a C-section made him nervous.

If you are considering an elective C-section, it is important to discuss your decision with your doctor early in your pregnancy. Elective C-sections can be scheduled starting at 39 weeks, but it is important to make arrangements as soon as possible to ensure availability at the hospital. Waiting too long could result in surgical suites being fully booked, and you may end up delivering after 39 weeks.

C-Section Risk to Baby

While a C-section delivery can be a lower risk to a baby as compared to a vaginal delivery, it is not risk-free. One of the most significant risks is the potential for breathing problems at birth. The baby must transition from fluid-filled lungs in the womb to air-filled lungs outside the womb in a short period, which can be challenging. This challenge is due, in part, to the lack of the squeezing action of the birth canal during a vaginal delivery that helps to expel fluid from the baby's lungs. As a result, babies born via cesarean delivery may have more difficulty clearing fluid from their lungs, increasing the risk of respiratory problems at birth.

C-Section Risk to Mom

During your pregnancy, you should have a discussion with your doctor about the risks of a C-section specific to you. Keep in mind that a C-section is a major abdominal surgery, and if you have any underlying medical issues, the risks may be even greater.

In an uncomplicated pregnancy, your doctor will likely discuss the possibility of the following risks associated with a C-section:

- Possible injury to the bowel or urinary system during the surgery.
- Infection at the incision site or inside the uterus.
- The need for a blood transfusion due to blood loss during the procedure.
- The possibility of a hysterectomy if there is severe bleeding or other complications.

While the risks of a C-section are relatively rare, occurring in less than 1 percent of cesarean deliveries according to one study of 30,000 pregnancies, the likelihood of complications may increase with the number of cesarean deliveries a mother has had.[4] For example, a woman who has had multiple C-sections may be at higher risk for placenta accrete or placenta previa in subsequent pregnancies. Additionally, there may be an increased risk of placental abruption, a serious pregnancy complication in which the placenta separates from the uterine wall before delivery.

When it comes to the number of cesarean deliveries a woman can have, there is no definitive answer or magic number. Medical evidence and studies do not support a specific number or range of numbers for the maximum number of C-sections a woman can safely have.

---

4   "Short- and Long-Term Outcomes after Cesarean Section," Medscape, March 24, 2011, https://www.medscape.com/viewarticle/739458_4.

C-Section Benefits

A C-section can spare the mother from potential vaginal trauma associated with a natural delivery. When a baby is delivered vaginally, there can be damage to the nerves, muscles, and connective tissue in the vaginal area. This can lead to issues such as urinary and bowel incontinence or pelvic organ prolapse, especially in women over the age of 30 or those delivering larger babies. Studies have shown that women over 30 are more likely to experience pelvic issues due to the vagina not bouncing back as easily as it did in their 20s.[5] Similarly, delivering a baby that weighs over 4000 grams (8.8 lbs) also increases the risk of pelvic issues.

C-Section Incisions

The two most common types of incisions are the horizontal lower transverse incision and the vertical midline incision. The lower transverse incision is typically used in non-emergency and elective C-sections because it has a lower risk of complications and allows for a faster recovery time. However, if the baby is in distress and needs to be delivered quickly, a vertical incision may be necessary.

---

5   Åsa Leijonhufvud et al., "Risk of Surgically Managed Pelvic Floor Dysfunction in Relation to Age at First Delivery," *American Journal of Obstetrics and Gynecology* 207, no. 4 (October 2012), https://doi.org/10.1016/j.ajog.2012.08.019.

Role of the Anesthesiologist

To ensure that you do not experience pain during a C-section, an anesthesiologist is usually required. There are two ways to achieve this. The first is through an epidural, which numbs you from the waist down while allowing you to remain awake during the procedure. Though you may feel some pressure, you should not feel any pain. It is important to note that the pressure you may feel in your upper abdomen or chest area as the baby is maneuvered out of you is a normal sensation, as it is not possible to numb your chest area. Once again, it is pressure, not pain.

The second option is general anesthesia, which involves placing an IV in your arm and administering anesthetic into your bloodstream to put you to sleep. This requires intubation to ensure you continue to breathe properly during the procedure. This method is typically reserved for emergencies where the baby needs to be delivered as soon as possible. Although the idea of waking up with a baby sounds appealing, general anesthesia is not recommended unless absolutely necessary.

There have been cases where the situation is dire, and the anesthesiologist cannot arrive at the hospital in time. In such cases, doctors at small hospitals may use a local anesthetic to numb the incision area and proceed with the C-section to deliver the baby as quickly as possible. While the local anesthesia may not be as effective, it is a necessary compromise in emergency situations.

Mental Psyche Vaginal Delivery versus C-Section

When you are in labor and experiencing painful contractions, your body is flooded with adrenaline, and all you can think about is getting your baby out. It is a natural response to pain, similar to when you instinctively pull away from something hot to stop the sensation and prevent further injury. This is because our body's natural response to pain is to avoid or escape it, and labor is no exception to this rule. By focusing on the goal of delivering your little one so the pain stops, you overcome the realization that you are about to deliver a baby.

A C-section is a different experience altogether. You do not go into labor and initiate this normal response to pain. The process of a C-section can feel surreal, as you know that your baby will soon be born, but you may not have the same physical cues as you would with labor contractions. Instead, you may feel a mix of emotions, such as nervousness, excitement, and a sense of eerie calmness. Unlike labor, where the primary focus is on getting the baby out to relieve the pain, C-section moms do not have that overwhelming feeling. Instead, they must rely on the excitement of knowing they are about to meet their little one very soon.

Keep in mind that a C-section is a quick and relatively straightforward procedure once you enter the operating room. Within a short time, you will be able to meet your newborn baby.

Chapter 14
Pitocin in Labor

Pitocin is a medication that helps increase contractions and aids in the baby's descent through the birth canal. It is often abbreviated as "Pit" instead of being pronounced in full. Pitocin is used for two purposes during childbirth: induction and augmentation. Induction is the process of starting labor, where Pitocin is used to stimulate contractions and bring on labor. Augmentation, on the other hand, is the process of speeding up or accelerating labor by improving the strength and frequency of contractions that are already occurring.

While Pitocin is commonly used and recommended by physicians, it is also the most common factor in legal cases related to childbirth. As with many things in medicine, there are benefits, risks, and potential complications associated with the use of Pitocin. This chapter aims to provide an overview of Pitocin, with a focus on its significance in the legal realm of childbirth.

High-Alert Medication

The Institute for Safe Medication Practices, an international organization, has identified Pitocin as one of the high-alert medications. This means that errors made with Pitocin can have devastating consequences for patients. In fact, Pitocin is one of only twelve medications in the world that have been included on this list.

Warnings for the Baby

The manufacturer of Pitocin has listed a range of adverse reactions that babies can experience as a result of the drug. These warnings can be found in the package insert for Pitocin and include: low heart rate in infants (bradycardia), seizures at birth, injury to the brain, and even death in some cases. It is worth noting that these side effects are seen in legal baby cases when Pitocin is used during labor and delivery.

Legal baby lawyers are acutely aware of the dangers of Pitocin, but some doctors may not be. In a case highlighting this issue, a doctor testified that she was unaware of the risks associated with Pitocin. Shockingly, she was not even aware that it was classified as a high-alert medication. She also admitted on the record that she had never reviewed the package insert for Pitocin. What is concerning is that this doctor had completed her residency only two years prior, indicating that her medical training may not be adequately addressing the dangers of Pitocin. It is important to note that other doctors and nurses have testified about the risks and dangers associated with Pitocin and that it is a high-alert medication. However, opinions on Pitocin can vary among medical professionals.

Does Pitocin Cause Autism?

It is worth noting that there is a debate regarding the potential relationship between Pitocin and autism. Some doctors believe that there may be a connection, while others disagree.[6] However, it is important for parents to be aware of this issue.

While some doctors believe there may be a link between Pitocin and autism, the American College of Obstetricians and Gynecologists (ACOG) does not support this view.[7] ACOG has advised doctors that it is unnecessary to inform patients of any studies that link autism and Pitocin. Therefore, your doctor may not bring up this issue during your pregnancy. If you are concerned about this potential link, you may need to conduct your own research or contact the doctors who performed the studies to obtain more information.

---

6   Melissa Smallwood et al., "Increased Risk of Autism Development in Children Whose Mothers Experienced Birth Complications or Received Labor and Delivery Drugs," *ASN Neuro* 8, no. 4 (2016): p. 175909141665974, https://doi.org/10.1177/1759091416659742.

7   "Labor Induction or Augmentation and Autism," ACOG, May 2014, https://www.acog.org/clinical/clinical-guidance/committee-opinion/articles/2014/05/labor-induction-or-augmentation-and-autism.

Warnings for Mom

Pitocin can cause several common side effects, such as nausea, vomiting, and stomach pain, as well as water retention. However, the most significant warning for mothers is related to higher doses of the drug or if the uterus is sensitive to it. This can cause contractions to last longer than usual, which can increase unnecessary stress on the baby during labor.

According to the drug insert, Pitocin has been associated with maternal deaths due to hypertensive episodes, subarachnoid hemorrhage, and rupture of the uterus during its use for labor induction in the first and second stages of labor. It is essential to be aware of these potential risks and discuss them with your doctor before deciding to use Pitocin during labor.

Elective Pitocin Induction at 39 Weeks

The label for Pitocin clearly states that the drug is not intended for elective labor inductions. This contradicts the widespread belief among doctors that inducing labor with Pitocin at 39 weeks without any medical necessity is acceptable. In 2018, a study called ARRIVE was conducted and published in the New England Journal of Medicine.[8] It found that inducing labor with Pitocin at 39 weeks did not have any adverse effects on either the baby or the mother. In fact, the study suggested that inducing labor at 39 weeks with Pitocin could lower the risk of C-sections.

---

8   "Labor Induction versus Expectant Management in Low-Risk Nulliparous ...," accessed February 21, 2023, https://www.nejm.org/doi/10.1056/NEJMoa1800566.

Based on these findings, the American College of Obstetricians and Gynecologists (ACOG) issued a statement in 2018 suggesting that elective induction with Pitocin at 39 weeks' gestation is a reasonable option. This means that your doctor can offer you this option during your pregnancy.

Protocols for Scheduled Inductions

If you are going to have a scheduled induction, many doctors have a standard approach. One concern with this approach is that they are not individualized for the patient. For example, a doctor testified in a baby case that he has a standard protocol where he admits patients in the evening, gives them Cytotec to ripen their cervix, and then goes home for the night while ordering the nurse to give a second dose of Cytotec. He orders Pitocin at 6:00 a.m. the following morning, orders it to be increased at 6:30 a.m., and comes into the hospital to check on the patient and break their water if possible at 7:00 a.m. before going to his office for the day.

This protocol is anything but individualized patient care. Not everyone responds the same way to cervical ripening. The nurse may give a second dose of Cytotec when it is not needed, and starting Pitocin at an arbitrary time may not be the best option for every patient. In some cases, waiting another couple of hours could be more beneficial. This generic approach does not account for such individualized factors. It is important to have a personalized induction plan that takes into account your specific needs and concerns.

Pro Tip

Make sure your elective induction is specific to you from start to finish. Everyone responds to Pitocin and cervical ripening differently. Generic orders from your doctor without regard to how you are progressing are a risk to you and your baby. This should be discussed with your doctor during the pregnancy once you have made the decision to undergo an elective induction of labor.

Pitocin Affects Everyone Differently

It is essential to understand that every mother's response to Pitocin during labor can vary significantly. As per the Pitocin package insert, the response to Pitocin is "individualized," and how a person reacts to it can depend on the sensitivity of their uterus, their genes, and their natural oxytocin levels.

As a result, the appropriate amount of Pitocin given to a mother during labor should be adjusted to suit their individual needs. Similarly, the duration of labor can vary significantly from one mother to another during an induction, and this should be taken into account as well.

Pro Tip

If it is your first-time receiving Pitocin, no one knows how you are going to react to the drug. Unless there is a medical reason to do otherwise, starting at a low dose with slow increases will help you and your delivery team asses your response to the Pitocin.

How Much Pitocin Do I Get?

To administer Pitocin, healthcare providers measure it in milliunits per minute (mU/min). Starting Pitocin requires a doctor's order, which typically outlines the starting dose, the frequency and amount of dosage increases, and when to stop increasing the drug.

How Much Pitocin to Start?
It is common for doctors to start Pitocin induction at a dosage of 1 to 2 mU/min. However, the Pitocin package insert recommends a lower starting dose, ranging from 0.05 to 1.0 mU/min.

How Much Is Pitocin Increased?
The typical doctor's order and the Pitocin package insert recommend increasing the dosage by 1 or 2 mU/min. For example, if the initial dosage is 1 mU/min, it may be increased to 2 mU/min, then 3 mU/min, and so on. If the dosage is being increased by twos, it may be increased to 2 mU/min, then 4 mU/min, and then 6 mU/min.

It is also worth noting that one study found Pitocin can cause stronger than usual contractions and reduced blood flow to the uterus and therefore, the baby.[9] This decrease in blood flow, and therefore oxygen to the baby, was noted to increase the risk of harm to the baby. The study determined

---

9   Springer. Olsson et al., "Maternal and newborn plasma oxytocin levels in response to maternal synthetic oxytocin administration during labour, birth and postpartum – a systematic review with implications for the function of the oxytocinergic," BMC Pregnancy Childbirth 23 (2023): 137.

that the adverse reactions to the baby were more likely to occur with higher dosages of Pitocin. Therefore, the study concluded that Pitocin should run at the "lowest possible infusion rates."

Pro Tip

The slower Pitocin increases of 1 mU/min (rather than 2 mU/min) may reduce the likelihood of excessive contractions and help ensure that the optimal dosage is achieved without overstimulating the uterus.

How Often Is Pitocin Increased?

Traditionally, doctors have recommended increasing the dosage of Pitocin every 30 minutes to induce or augment labor. However, the Pitocin package insert recommends waiting at least 30 to 60 minutes before increasing the dosage.

Several studies have evaluated the "steady state" of Pitocin and its effect on uterine contractions.[10,11] It has been found that it takes anywhere from 20 to 90 minutes for Pitocin to reach a steady state and for the uterus to achieve its maximum response to the drug.

---

10   Joseph Seitchik et al., "Oxytocin Augmentation of Dysfunctional Labor," *American Journal of Obstetrics and Gynecology* 150, no. 3 (October 1984): pp. 225-228

11   Ransom, Justin L., et al. "Steady-state oxytocin concentrations after continuous intravenous infusion in term and preterm neonates." *Journal of Perinatology* 36, no. 8 (2016): 645-649.

Pro Tip

The 20-to-90-minute variation it takes for your body to respond to Pitocin underscores the importance of monitoring how you are responding to the drug before increasing the dosage. By watching the body's response to the drug, your nurse can tailor the dosage specifically to your labor and reduce the risk of adverse effects. When the Pitocin should be increased should depend on your specific labor and response to the Pitocin, regardless of what the generic doctor order may state.

When Will They Stop Increasing Pitocin?

The goal is to achieve a steady and effective contraction pattern that promotes labor progression. To achieve an adequate contraction pattern during labor, the typical approach is to increase the Pitocin dosage until you are having three to five contractions within a ten-minute period. These contractions should be strong, lasting 40 to 90 seconds each, and there should be cervical change. Once adequate contractions are established, the nurse may choose to maintain or decrease the Pitocin dosage.

Pro Tip

In the legal baby cases, a big issue is when the nurse should have stopped increasing the Pitocin as the patient was adequately contracting. This is an area where doctors and nurses disagree. This means different delivery teams will make different decisions on whether to increase or decrease the Pitocin.

Make sure you are comfortable with every increase and your delivery teams' approach to the induction.

What Is the Maximum Pitocin Dosage I Should Get in Labor?

The recommended maximum dosage of Pitocin varies between typical doctor's orders and the Pitocin package insert. According to the package insert, a dosage of 6 mU/min can produce the same effect as natural or spontaneous labor. The package insert recommends using higher doses with caution and only in rare circumstances, with a maximum dosage of 9-10 mU/min. In contrast, the typical doctor's order may allow for increasing Pitocin up to 20 mU/min, with a second order needed to increase it further to 30 mU/min.

One study found that when mom gets Pitocin in labor, her body produces more of the natural hormone called oxytocin.[12] Pitocin is a man-made version of the hormone oxytocin, which is naturally produced by the body. If doctors give a low amount of Pitocin (less than 10 milliunits per minute), the mom's oxytocin levels stay the same as they would during natural labor. However, when doctors give high amounts of Pitocin over 10 mU/min (up to 32 mU/min), the mom's oxytocin levels can become two to three times higher than normal. This can put your body into Pitocin/oxytocin

---

12 Springer. Olsson et al., "Maternal and newborn plasma oxytocin levels in response to maternal synthetic oxytocin administration during labour, birth and postpartum – a systematic review with implications for the function of the oxytocinergic," BMC Pregnancy Childbirth 23 (2023): 137.

overdrive. As pointed out in the study, this can lead to several complications for both the mom and the baby.

It is crucial to understand that the response to Pitocin is highly individualized, meaning that the appropriate dose will vary for each patient. While some moms may require a lower dose, others may need a higher amount of Pitocin. However, it is essential to note that giving higher doses of Pitocin, exceeding the recommended amount stated in the package insert of 9-10 mU/min, has been associated with complications and is often seen in legal baby cases. Therefore, if you pass the magic number 10mu/min, make sure your team is carefully monitoring your response to the Pitocin and adjusting the dosage to avoid any adverse effects.

Pro Tip

Higher doses of Pitocin can pose significant risks to both you and your baby during the induction. To minimize these risks, you can take an active role in your induction process by requesting that your doctor limit the Pitocin dose to a maximum of 10 mU/min. This way, if your delivery team wants to increase the dose beyond this limit, they must first obtain an order from your doctor. This will trigger a discussion about the specifics of your induction, including whether it is truly necessary to exceed the 10 mU/min limit.

When Pitocin Should Be Decreased or Stopped

There are two primary reasons to stop or decrease Pitocin:

- Excessive contractions: Contractions that occur with every 1 to 2 minutes or over five in 10 minutes.
- Concerns about the baby's heart rate: A sign that the baby is not tolerating the stress from contractions.

Pro Tip

There is a significant disagreement among doctors in the legal baby world as to when Pitocin should be stopped or decreased in response to the baby's heart rate or too many contractions. Given this disagreement, it is essential that your delivery team prioritize caution during your induction. Baby always gets the benefit of the doubt when there are any concerns, which may equal turning the Pitocin down or off.

Hospitals Have Pitocin Policies

Hospital policies vary on the use of Pitocin during labor and delivery, and they provide guidelines for your delivery team on how to administer the drug. These policies typically specify the initial dose, the rate of increase, the frequency of adjustments, and the maximum dose to be given. Your nurse is typically the most knowledgeable person about the hospital's protocol, as they will be responsible for managing the administration of Pitocin. It is important to discuss the policy with your nurse, including when and under what circumstances Pitocin should be discontinued or reduced. This can help you better understand what to expect during labor and how the use of Pitocin will be managed by your nurse.

Contractions Are Key: Internal Monitor/IUPC

When Pitocin is used to stimulate contractions, the frequency of contractions is crucial in determining the appropriate dosage. There are different ways to monitor contractions, including external and internal monitors, or an IUPC. While an external monitor is placed on the skin and assesses contractions through the abdominal wall, an IUPC is inserted into the uterus beside the baby and provides more accurate measurement of your contractions. This can help reduce the risk of excessive contractions.

Using an IUPC also allows your delivery team to calculate the Montevideo units (MVUs), which measure the pressure of the contractions over a 10-minute period. A normal range for MVUs is 200 to 250. If your MVUs are above this normal range, it could indicate that your contractions are too strong, and Pitocin may need to be adjusted. You can ask your delivery team to calculate the Montevideo units to help you determine if your contractions are too strong.

The Nurse's Story: Safe versus Unsafe Hospital for Pitocin

A nurse left her previous job at an "unsafe hospital" due, in part, to concerns about how Pitocin inductions were being managed. She began working at a new hospital that she considered to be "safe," where Pitocin inductions were handled differently than at her previous workplace.

• At the unsafe hospital, nurses were assigned to two patients that were on Pitocin at the same time, while at the safe hospital, nurses were assigned to only one patient undergoing a Pitocin induction. This ensured that patients received one-on-one care during the induction of labor.

• At the unsafe hospital, the dosage of Pitocin was increased by 2 mU/min every 30 minutes until it reached 20 milliunits/minute. This high dosage was commonly reached. In contrast, at the safe hospital, the dosage was only increased by 1 mU/min and longer periods of time were allowed to pass before increasing it. As a result, the safe hospital rarely increased the dosage to the high teens and never reached 20 mU/min.

The nurse explained that when Pitocin is increased slowly and in increments of one, the "sweet spot" is not missed. This refers to the ideal dosage of Pitocin that is just right for the patient, neither too little nor too much. The safe hospital aimed to achieve this goal, and as a result, the nurse reported that they did not encounter the same issues with Pitocin inductions that the unsafe hospital.

Pro Tip

This story highlights the critical importance of selecting the right hospital for yourself and your baby if you plan on undergoing a Pitocin induction. Even if you live in a rural area with limited options, it is essential to discuss with your doctor ahead of time the measures necessary to ensure the safest possible induction, such as setting specific parameters similar to those in the safe hospital described in the story. Be proactive by talking to your doctor about what you want and what they recommend. It is important that you are on the same page as your doctor before starting the Pitocin induction.

Who Is Running the Show with a Pitocin Induction?

The induction process is typically overseen by a nurse who is responsible for updating the doctor and carrying out their orders, including starting, increasing, decreasing, and stopping the Pitocin as necessary. While the nurse may consult with the doctor about Pitocin increases in some cases, they generally have a high degree of autonomy during the induction process.

Should the Doctor Break My Water?

Breaking your water can be an effective way to jumpstart labor, particularly when done during a Pitocin induction. This approach may even alleviate the need for increasing Pitocin, particularly if the mother has had a prior vaginal delivery. In fact, some doctors are known for decreasing the Pitocin after a patient's water breaks.

However, if the goal is to shorten labor, a combination of Pitocin and breaking the bag of water may be preferred. Ultimately, the decision to break your water during an induction will depend on a variety of factors specific to your labor and what your doctor recommends.

Is My Cervix Ready for Pitocin?

Before proceeding with the induction, your physician will evaluate your cervix to determine if it is favorable or unfavorable. To do this, they may use a scoring system called the Bishop score, which assesses five factors: cervical dilation, cervical effacement, cervical consistency (whether the cervix is firm, medium, or soft), fetal station (how far down the birth canal the baby has descended), and cervical position. The most significant factor in the Bishop score is cervical dilation. A higher Bishop score indicates a more favorable cervix and a greater likelihood of a successful induction. There is also a simplified version of the Bishop score that only evaluates dilation, effacement, and fetal station. By assessing your Bishop score, your doctor can determine whether induction is likely to be successful and whether your cervix needs to be ripened.

Ripening the Cervix for Pitocin

If your cervix is found to be unfavorable for induction, your doctors may want to ripen it first. This process involves softening, thinning, and dilating the cervix to prepare it for a successful induction using Pitocin. There are several ways to ripen the cervix, which include:

1. *The Balloon*

    This involves placing a deflated balloon through your cervix and into your uterus, and then filling it with saline to apply pressure on the cervix. The part that fills the balloon with saline is typically taped to your inner thigh. While this method can be uncomfortable, it is considered a more natural approach.

    It is worth noting that doctors will typically not use this method if your bag of water has already broken. The balloon is left in place until it falls out on its own or until around 12 hours have passed, whichever comes first. Pitocin may be started either when the balloon is inserted or after it has been removed.

2. *Cytotec (Warning)*

    Cytotec is a pill placed inside the vagina or taken orally. Since it comes in a pill form, the dosage cannot be decreased or stopped. Pitocin cannot be administered until 4 to 6 hours after the last dose of Cytotec if it is done vaginally, or 2 hours if taken orally.

Pro Tip

It is important to note that Cytotec is not recommended for use in VBAC (vaginal birth after C-section) deliveries, as it can increase the risk of uterine rupture. In fact, the FDA has issued warnings about using it in labor due to its potential risks to both mothers and babies. This is an upgrade from their initial recommendation of not using it at all during an induction of labor. It is also worth noting that many nurses have expressed their dislike for the drug, and it has been involved in legal cases related to childbirth.

Despite these concerns, hospitals continue to use Cytotec because it is cost-effective. If considering Cytotec, know that different dosages are available, with experts recommending a half dose (25 micrograms) instead of the full dose (50 micrograms). One study found that the half dose was just as effective as the full dose.[13] If you are considering induction and your doctor suggests Cytotec, it is important to discuss other options for ripening your cervix and weigh the potential risks and benefits of each option.

3. *Cervidil and Prepidil*

Cervidil is similar to a tampon and can be easily removed by the delivery team if necessary. Cervidil is a timed-release method that slowly releases the medication, preventing overstimulation of the uterus. If it does start to cause too many contractions, they pull it out similar to a tampon. Cervidil is left in place until active labor starts or for up to 12 hours. Pitocin can be started 30 minutes after Cervidil is removed. In some countries, Cervidil is even used for moms who had a previous C-section.

Prepidil is another option that comes in the form of a gel placed in the vagina. It can be repeated every 6 to 12 hours until adequate uterine activity is achieved. Pitocin

---

13   M.M. Meydanli et al., "Labor Induction Post-Term with 25 Micrograms vs. 50 Micrograms of Intravaginal Misoprostol," *International Journal of Gynecology &Amp; Obstetrics* 81, no. 3 (April 26, 2003): pp. 249-255, https://doi.org/10.1016/s0020-7292(03)00042-0.

cannot be started for 6 to 12 hours after the final dose. Although Cervidil and Prepidil are preferred by some healthcare professionals, they are more expensive than Cytotec.

Changing Plans during the Induction

If at any point you are not comfortable with your induction of labor, speak up and communicate your concerns to your physician. For instance, if you notice any irregularities in your baby's heart rate or experience adverse effects in response to Pitocin, do not hesitate to discuss your options with your doctor. They may suggest reducing the Pitocin dosage, taking a break from the medication (if it is medically feasible), or even proceeding with a C-section delivery. In the same way, if your physician is worried about how your baby is responding to Pitocin, they may suggest alternative plans for delivery. Keep in mind that the ultimate goal is a safe and healthy delivery for you and your baby, so you may have to go to Plan B.

Pitocin Dosages Are Different in Almost Every Country

It is important to note that Pitocin dosages can vary significantly between different countries due to the lack of a consensus on the optimal starting point for the drug. The initial doses of Pitocin can range from as low as 0.5 mU/min to as high as 6 mU/min, with increasing ranges from 10 to 60 minutes and maximum doses ranging from 16 to 64 mU/min. If you plan to leave the United States during your pregnancy, keep in mind that the management approach to Pitocin may differ in other countries.

Stressed-Out Baby before Pitocin Induction

In the introduction story, Sam arrived at the hospital and the fetal monitor showed that her baby was not doing well. Sam then had to make the difficult decision to induce labor, which put additional stress on her baby. Although Sam's story had a positive outcome, unfortunately, not all similar stories do.

When mom arrives at the hospital carrying a baby with a concerning heart rate, it is often an indication that the baby had been under stress prior to arriving at the hospital. It is difficult to determine how long this has been going on or what is causing the stress on a baby. In such cases, patients are typically presented with the option of a C-section or possibly a Pitocin induction. Keep in mind that a Pitocin induction will place further stress on the baby, which can be a problem if the baby cannot tolerate the contractions. There have been legal cases where this exact scenario has played out. They start the Pitocin, and the baby does not respond well, ultimately resulting in an emergency C-section. Although the baby may have arrived in distress, the argument in legal baby cases is that the use of Pitocin made the situation worse for the baby.

Pro Tip
If your doctor is inducing labor due to concerns about your baby's heart rate or health, it is crucial to closely monitor

your baby's condition throughout the process. A trusted family member or friend can act as a baby advocate and keep a watchful eye on the fetal heart rate monitor.

Successful Pitocin Induction

If your doctor recommends a Pitocin induction and you agree, it is crucial to be well-informed about the induction to avoid any complications. To help you, I have put together the following 14 tips, which are based on legal cases that arose from mistakes made during a labor induction.

Top 14 Tips for a Successful Pitocin Induction

1. **Consider using an internal fetal monitor.**

    Consider requesting an internal monitor to accurately measure your baby's heart rate and contractions after your water breaks. Hospital policies may permit the use of external and wireless monitors during Pitocin inductions, but an internal monitor is the most accurate.

2. **Know how to read your baby's heart rate and contraction pattern.**

    If Pitocin is causing too many contractions and it is putting too much stress on your baby, you will know by looking at their heart rate. It is important to watch your contractions and see how the baby is responding to them. If their heart rate slows down while you are having a contraction, your baby may be struggling with contractions.

3. **Be alert during shift changes.**

   When your delivery team is getting off work and giving a report to the oncoming delivery team, it can be a little chaotic as the new team learns about the patients on the labor and delivery floor.

4. **Have a baby advocate in the room at all times.**

   Nurses will typically have other patients and responsibilities while you are on Pitocin, particularly if the unit is busy. A second set of eyes on your baby's heart rate and contractions is critical when Pitocin is running.

5. **Know what concerning signs and symptoms to report to your delivery team.**

   Report any adverse reactions to Pitocin, such as headache, nausea, vomiting, abdominal pain, or drowsiness, to your delivery team immediately so they can adjust the Pitocin if necessary. If you are having increased abdominal pain to the point that you are requesting an epidural or they are giving you more anesthesia in your epidural due to pain, this may also be a sign that the Pitocin needs to be turned down or turned off.

6. **The magic number ten. Know your doctor's Pitocin order.**

   Pitocin orders vary from one doctor to the next. Make sure you know what your doctor is ordering for your Pitocin induction. Are they starting at .5,

1 or 2 mU/min, and how often is the nurse being ordered to increase the Pitocin?

As higher doses of Pitocin can pose significant risks to both you and your baby during induction, consider requesting that your doctor limit the Pitocin dose to a maximum of 10 mU/min. If you need a higher dose of Pitocin past 10 mU/min, your nurse can call your doctor, discuss your induction, and get a second order to increase the Pitocin past 10 mU/min.

7. **Know how much Pitocin is running at all times.**

    Ask the nurse to tell you when she is increasing Pitocin. Sometimes, doctors and nurses disagree on when Pitocin should be increased. Make sure you are communicating with your nurse and get their opinion on the increase. They are the ones at your bedside, observing you and reviewing your baby's heart rate, so their opinion is important.

8. **Consider a slow and steady Pitocin induction.**

    Consider keeping the Pitocin low and increasing it gradually to avoid missing the "sweet spot," which is the optimal dose of Pitocin to ensure you do not have too many contractions. Keep in mind that no one knows how you will respond to Pitocin, unless you have had a prior induction. Taking the slow and steady route will help you determine how your body responds to the drug without overloading your baby with too many contractions.

9. **Ask about the hospital policy or protocol for labor induction and when Pitocin should be stopped or decreased per the protocol.**

    The nurse will not give you a copy of the hospital Pitocin protocol, as they are internal documents. However, the nurse should be familiar with the policy and can verbally explain it to you. The most significant part of the policy is when the nurse will stop Pitocin in response to the baby's heart rate or contractions. This will give you and your baby advocate an idea of how your nurse should respond if your baby is struggling with Pitocin.

10. **Request one-on-one nursing care with a Pitocin induction.**

    Nurses that have two patients on Pitocin at the same time have described this as unsafe. They do not have the air support at the hospital to safely manage two patients on Pitocin simultaneously. Depending on the hospital, one-on-one care may be standard, but at other hospitals, it is not. If your nurse does have two patients in labor on Pitocin, your baby advocate will play a very important role in your labor.

11. **Decreasing Pitocin if your water breaks during the induction.**

    If your water breaks, whether it happens naturally or the delivery team assists in breaking it, it is worth discussing with them the possibility of reducing or stop increasing the Pitocin. You can take a moment to observe how your body responds without additional or a reduced amount of Pitocin. It is possible that you may be able to progress in labor without any further increases, particularly if you have already had a vaginal delivery.

12. **Keep the Pitocin dose low if you have had multiple vaginal deliveries.**

    In some legal cases where the mom had too many contractions from the Pitocin, it has caused her uterus to tear open or the placenta to detach from the uterine wall. In these cases, the moms had multiple vaginal births. One doctor explained that the uterus gets "tired," and the tissue in the uterus changes after multiple births. This means it becomes important to ensure mom is not contracting too much if she has had multiple vaginal deliveries.

13. **Contractions are key: watch them closely.**

    If you are experiencing contractions every 1 to 2 minutes or more than 5 in a 10-minute period, this is considered too many contractions when you are on Pitocin, particularly if it lasts more than 30 minutes.

14. **Find out your nurse's experience with Pitocin inductions.**

    Pitocin inductions can be tricky, especially for those who lack experience. If the nurse keeps the Pitocin dosage low and increases it gradually, their lack of experience may not be as concerning. However, if an inexperienced nurse increases the Pitocin dosage to 16, 18, or 20 mU/min within a shorter period of time, this would be very concerning.

Nursing Mothers

It is important to note that according to the package insert for Pitocin, there is a possibility that the drug can be transmitted through breast milk to the baby, although it is unclear to what extent. As with many other medications, caution is advised for breastfeeding mothers who have received Pitocin during labor. Several studies have found detectable levels of Pitocin in the breastmilk of lactating women who received Pitocin during labor, including a 2014 study published in the *Journal of Obstetric, Gynecologic, and Neonatal Nursing*.[14] Therefore, it is important for breastfeeding mothers to discuss with their healthcare provider the potential risks and benefits of using Pitocin during labor and its possible impact on breastfeeding.

---

14 Jardine, L. A., Foureur, M. J., & Turnbull, D. (2014). A survey of intrapartum synthetic oxytocin use in New South Wales hospitals, 2011. Journal of Obstetric, Gynecologic, and Neonatal Nursing, 43(1), 91-101.

Chapter 15

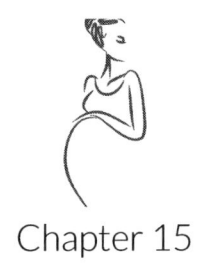

A Perfect Gift from God

On a beautiful day, I found myself at a wedding amidst the excitement of writing this book. The sun was shining bright as I walked into the wedding venue. The guests were all seated, eagerly awaiting the arrival of the bridal party and the newly married couple. As I made my way to my seat, I could hear the sound of music in the background, getting louder and louder.

The DJ turned up the music, as it was time to welcome the bridal party. As the DJ announced their arrival, the guests stood up, clapping and cheering as the group made their way to the front of the room. The bride and groom followed shortly after, hand in hand, and their smiles lit up the room. It was the perfect start to an unforgettable night.

As the music faded and everyone settled into their seats, the groom's father stepped up to the microphone. He spoke with warmth and sincerity as he congratulated the newlyweds, expressing his gratitude for being a part of their special day. The groom's father continued to share his excitement about the merging of two families, and how it was a time to create even more happy memories together.

The groom's father captivated the entire room with his heartfelt words as he recounted the day his son was born. With vivid detail, he transported us all back to that special moment when he held his newborn son for the first time. He spoke of his overwhelming love and joy as he remembered staring at his son for the first time, and thinking that he was the "perfect gift from God." As he shared these words, a wave of emotion spread throughout the room, and tears filled the eyes of many. The atmosphere was charged with nostalgia, with every parent in the room remembering their own special moment with their children. It was a moment of connection and shared experience, and it left a mark on all who were present that day. As I wiped away my own tears, I knew exactly how I would finish this book.

The journey of labor is undoubtedly one of the most beautiful experiences that any mother can go through. The anticipation and excitement of welcoming a new life into the world are matched only by the sense of wonder and amazement at the miracle of childbirth.

As you go through the journey of labor, keep your mind focused on what is to come—welcoming your little one into the world and the joy they will bring to your family. Take deep breaths and remind yourself that the beauty and magic of childbirth is right around the corner. Every contraction signifies progress toward that moment when you can finally hold your baby in your arms. The rush of emotions that will overcome you as you lock eyes with your newborn for the first time, the feeling of their tiny hand wrapped around your finger, the warmth of their body as they lie in your arms.

Hold on to this vision as you go through labor, knowing that this surreal and beautiful experience is within your reach. The moment when everything else fades away, and your heart fills with love and joy. It is a moment like no other, and you will want it to last forever as you hold your perfect gift from God.

Additional Resources and Information

Please visit my website at ginamundy.com for more additional information about this book and my mission to help families have a healthy baby.

Your feedback is incredibly important to me. If you have any questions, comments, or personal experiences you would like to share, I encourage you to reach out to me directly at gm@ginamundy.com. The email will go to my phone, and I will personally respond. I am here to provide support and continue the conversation beyond the pages of this book.

Thank you for taking the time to read my book. I wish you a safe and smooth delivery, and a lifetime of joy and happiness with your precious baby.

Acknowledgments

I would like to express my heartfelt gratitude to everyone who contributed to the creation of this book and supported me throughout the process. Your assistance and encouragement were invaluable, and I am forever grateful.

First and foremost, I want to thank my niece, Samantha LaFrance, for graciously allowing me to share her story as the introduction to this book. Your openness and willingness to share your experiences will undoubtedly help parents understand the decisions they may face during pregnancy and childbirth.

I am also deeply grateful to Ali Perez for allowing me to use her story as an example of the power of a baby advocate. Your journey has showcased the importance of advocating for the well-being of our little ones.

To the individuals who provided professional guidance, I extend my sincere appreciation. Jeannie Culbertson, thank you for being there from the beginning to the end, guiding me throughout the entire process. Your expertise and support were invaluable.

I would also like to express my gratitude to Allison Rose, who helped me shape this book into its final form. Your input and advice played a crucial role in bringing this project to life.

A special mention goes to Stephanie Parent, whose insightful final thoughts and thorough review ensured that the book was ready for publication. Your dedication and attention to detail have been instrumental in refining the content.

I would like to extend my heartfelt appreciation to Edna Cucksey Stephens for her invaluable contribution to this book. Her keen eye and expertise played a pivotal role in completing the book. With her exceptional attention to detail, she swooped in with last-minute tweaks that made a significant difference in the final manuscript.

To my family and friends, thank you for understanding and supporting me, even though it meant I spent a lot less time with you the past 14 months. Your patience and encouragement have meant the world to me.

To my daughters and son, I hope the guidance in this book will serve as a valuable resource when the time comes for you to experience the miracle of childbirth. I appreciate your understanding and independence as you took care of yourselves, managed household chores, and tended to the needs of our furry friends.

I would like to express my deep gratitude to my husband, James Mundy. Your unwavering support and remarkable qualities go far beyond your good looks; you possess a heart of pure gold. I am immensely thankful to you for graciously affording me the time and space needed to work on this project. Your selflessness shines through in the countless evenings you spent preparing meals, caring for our children, and ensuring their peaceful nights. You have been my pillar of strength throughout this incredible journey, and I sincerely acknowledge that I could not have accomplished this without you.

I would like to express my gratitude to my incredible mother-in-law, Susan Mundy. Throughout the years, you have been a pillar of support, always there to lend a helping hand as our children were growing up. Your invaluable assistance enabled me to travel across the country, sometimes on a weekly basis, with the peace of mind that my children were in caring hands. Your presence in our lives has made all the difference, and I am deeply grateful for your love and support.

I would like to express my heartfelt appreciation to my sisters, Kelly Giampaola and April Gardner. They are not only my sisters but also my best friends. I am incredibly grateful for their love and support throughout this journey. I have enjoyed the countless conversations we have shared about childbirth, which have enriched the content of this book.

To my nieces and nephews, who hold a special place in my heart, I want you to know that I cherish you as if you were my own children. It is my sincerest hope that this book will serve as a meaningful resource for you, guiding you with wisdom and love. Your presence in my life has brought immeasurable joy, and I am excited to share this book with you.

I extend my heartfelt thanks to my beta readers—Jade, Brittany, Gretchen, Meredith, Leslie, and Samantha—for investing their time in reading this book and providing valuable feedback during their own pregnancies. Your input helped shape the final product. A special mention goes to my mom, Susan Thomas, my number one beta reader. Your constant encouragement throughout each draft of the book, from beginning to end, has been a tremendous source of motivation.

In addition, I am truly grateful to Mark Kaiser for his captivating speech delivered at his son's wedding. The words you spoke resonated deeply with every guest in attendance, reminding us all of the significance of childbirth. Your heartfelt reminder served as a constant source of inspiration throughout the writing process, infusing my work with renewed purpose and passion.

Lastly, I want to acknowledge the families I have encountered over the years. Your stories have deeply touched me, and I have carried you in my prayers. As a mother, meeting you, hearing your experiences, and witnessing your unimaginable pain have profoundly impacted me. For the first three months of writing, memories of your stories flooded my mind each morning as tears filled my eyes. I could not escape the emotional toll that years of detachment from the legal baby world had taken on me. It is through this journey of writing, allowing these emotions to resurface, that I realized how strong each one of you are. I want you to know that your stories have fueled my determination to prevent such tragedies. May this book serve as a source of knowledge and guidance, and may it help spare other families from enduring the heartache you have faced.

About the Author

Gina Mundy is an attorney specializing in legal cases related to childbirth. With more than two decades of experience investigating and examining mistakes that occur during labor and delivery, she possesses a deep understanding of what can go wrong during childbirth.

Throughout her career Mrs. Mundy has traveled nationwide, engaging with healthcare professionals such as doctors, nurses, and midwives to explore all aspects of labor and delivery. These interactions have provided her with invaluable insights, enabling her to appreciate the diverse perspectives prevalent in different regions of the country. Collaborating with experts from various states, she has explored and analyzed the myriad of issues that can arise during labor and delivery, impacting both mother and baby.

Mrs. Mundy has conducted extensive research, meticulously analyzing, and dissecting countless studies pertaining to childbirth. This rigorous process was essential in equipping her with the necessary knowledge to undertake lengthy cross-examinations of a diverse array of experts. Through these examinations, she skillfully discerns their opinions on the errors that have occurred during labor and delivery. This has sharpened her knowledge allowing her to become highly proficient in the nuances of childbirth.

In her capacity as legal counsel, Mrs. Mundy has closely worked with delivery teams whose care has been questioned following adverse outcomes. She has spent thousands of hours meticulously scrutinizing cases, conducting interviews with delivery teams, and thoroughly examining medical records to gain an in-depth understanding of every decision made during labor and delivery.

Leveraging her wealth of experience and expertise, Mrs. Mundy has authored a book aimed at preventing the recurrence of common mistakes that are made in labor and delivery. This invaluable resource serves as a guide for expecting parents, equipping them with insights and guidance to navigate the journey of childbirth. By empowering parents with knowledge and understanding, Mrs. Mundy's book enables them to take steps to help avoid these life changing mistakes and have a healthy baby. Mrs. Mundy firmly believes that while we cannot change the past, we can certainly learn from it and take measures to prevent similar situations from occurring in the future.

Index

A

Are Epidurals Safe in Labor? 199
  Baby Advocate and the Epidural 202
    Pro Tip 203
  Do Epidurals Affect Labor Progress? 203
  Do Not Practice on Me 200
  Epidural Procedure and Monitoring 199
  Epidurals and Autism 206
  Intralipids 201
  Pitocin Induction and Epidural 204
  Test Dose 201
  Unplanned C-Section or Operative Delivery 203

Assessing Contractions
  MODERATE VARIABILITY DURING CONTRACTIONS 164

B

Best Hospital for Baby
  Should You Pick a Hospital Before Choosing Your Doctor
    Pro Tip 102

Busy Labor and Delivery Units
  Tips for Your Labor and Delivery 192

C

Cytotec (Warning)

259

Pro Tip 235

D

Decelerations in the Baby's Heart Rate
  Early Deceleration 150
  Late Deceleration 152
  Variable Deceleration 150
Delayed Delivery
  Tips for Your Labor and Delivery 196
Do Epidurals Affect Labor Progress?
  Pro Tip 204
Do I Need a Plan for Labor and Delivery?
  An LAD Plan Is More than Just a Plan 106
  LAD Plan and Your Delivery Team 111
  LAD Plan and Your Doctor 109
  No LAD Plans in Legal Baby Cases 111
  What to Put in Your LAD Plan 113
  When to Write the LAD Plan 112
Doppler or External Monitor
  Intermittent Monitoring during Labor
    Pro Tip 138

H

How Much Pitocin Do I Get?
  How Much Is Pitocin Increased? 225
  How Much Pitocin to Start? 225
  What Is the Maximum Pitocin Dosage I Should Get in Labor? 228
  When Will They Stop Increasing Pitocin? 227

How Much Pitocin Will They Give Me?
Pro Tip 229
How Often Is Pitocin Increased?
Pro Tip 227

I

Interpreting Variability
MINIMAL VARIABILITY\
   STRAIGHTER LINE WITH MINIMAL FLUCTUA-
   TIONS 148
MODERATE VARIABILITY WITH FLUCTUATIONS BE-
   TWEEN 5 TO 25 BPM 148

Interventions During Vaginal Birth 176
Assisted Vaginal Birth – Vacuum and Forceps 177
Episiotomy 176

Interventions to Help the Baby 173
Amnioinfusion 174
Intrauterine Resuscitative Measures 173
Shut Off Pitocin 175
Start a Tocolytic (Terbutaline) 175, 176, 177

L

Lack of Intervention
Tips for Your Labor and Delivery 188

Learning from the Legal Baby Cases to Avoid Future Mistakes 179
Busy Labor and Delivery Units 191
Delayed Delivery - The Baby's Heart Rate on the Fetal Monitor 195

Lack of Intervention 188

Meconium 185

Pitocin 179

Residents 189

Shift Changes 194

Umbilical Cord 184

Wrong Type of Fetal Monitor 187

Legal Cases

   Internal Monitor versus the Wireless Monitor

      Pro Tip #1 136

      Pro Tip #2 136

M

Meconium

   Tips for Your Labor and Delivery 185

MODERATE VARIABILITY DURING CONTRACTIONS

   BABY IS HANDLING THE STRESS OF THE CONTRACTIONS 164

   BABY IS UNDER TOO MUCH STRESS DURING CONTRACTIONS 164

Monitoring Your Baby during Labor

   The Gold Standard 131

      Doppler or External Monitor\
         Intermittent Monitoring during Labor 137

      External Monitor\ The Easiest 132

      Internal Monitor\ Gold Standard 132

      Legal Cases\

Internal Monitor versus the Wireless Monitor 134

Which Monitor Should Be Used in Your Labor? 139

Wireless Monitor\ New Technology 133

P

Pitocin

Tips for Your Labor and Delivery 180

Pitocin in Labor 219

Changing Plans during the Induction 237

Does Pitocin Cause Autism? 221

Elective Pitocin Induction Can Be Done at 39 Weeks 222

High-Alert Medication 220

Hospitals Have Pitocin Policies. 230

How Much Pitocin Do I Get? 225

Is My Cervix Ready for Pitocin? 234

Nursing Mothers 244

Pitocin Affects Everyone Differently 224

  Pro Tip 224

Pitocin Dosages Are Different in Almost Every Country 237

Ripening the Cervix for Pitocin 234

Scheduled Inductions 223

Should the Doctor Break My Water? 233

Stressed-Out Baby before Pitocin Induction 238

Successful Pitocin Induction 239

The Nurse's Story\ Safe versus Unsafe Hospital for Pitocin 231

Warnings for Mom 222

Warnings for the Baby 220

When Pitocin Should Be Decreased or Stopped 229

Who Is Running the Show with a Pitocin Induction? 233

Preparing Your Baby Advocate

Be Familiar with Fetal Monitoring 128

Discuss Your LAD Plan 126

Know the Art of Effective Communication 127

Provide Air Support for Good Decision-Making 128

Understand the Common Facts in Legal Baby Cases 128

R

Residents

Tips for Your Labor and Delivery 190

Ripening the Cervix for Pitocin

Cervidil and Prepidil 236

Cytotec (Warning) 235

The Balloon 235

S

Scheduled Inductions

Pro Tip 224

Shift Changes

Tips for Your Labor and Delivery 194

Stressed-Out Baby before Pitocin Induction

Pro Tip 238

Successful Pitocin Induction

Top 14 Tips for a Successful Pitocin Induction 239

T

Testing
    Determine How the Baby Is Doing
    Biophysical Profile (BPP) 168
    Contraction Stress Test 171
    Nonstress Test (NST) 168
    Scalp Stimulation 169
    Start an Internal Monitor 172
    Ultrasound 172
    Vibroacoustic Stimulation 170

Tests to Evaluate Baby's Well-Being and Interventions during Labor 167
    Interventions to Help the Baby 177
    Testing\ Determine How the Baby Is Doing 168

The Baby Advocate 119
    Preparing Your Baby Advocate 125
    Pro Tip 123
    The Remote Baby Advocate 125
    Your Baby Advocate 123

The Dream Team
    The Role of Your Delivery Team
        Anesthesiologist 64

The Nurse's Story
    Safe versus Unsafe Hospital for Pitocin
        Pro Tip 232

The Perfect Gift from God 245

Tips for Your Labor and Delivery

Water Breaking 183

U

Umbilical Cord

Tips for Your Labor and Delivery 184

Understanding the C-Section Option before and during Labor 207

Arriving at the Hospital\

C-Section versus Vaginal Delivery 207

C- Section Benefits 215

C-Section Incisions 215

C-Section Risk to Baby 213

C-Section Risk to Mom 213

Elective C-Sections 212

Emergency C-Section 211

Mental Psyche Vaginal Delivery versus C-Section 217

Role of the Anesthesiologist 216

V

Variability or Fluctuations in the Baseline

Absent Variability 147

Marked Variability 147

Minimal Variability 146

Moderate Variability 146

Variable Deceleration

SINGLE VARIABLE DECELERATION 151

TWO VARIABLE DECELERATIONS HAPPENING WITH EVERY OTHER CONTRACTION 152

W

Water Breaking
  Tips for Your Labor and Delivery 183
What to Put in Your LAD Plan
  10 Things to Consider When Preparing an LAD Plan 114
What You Need to Know about Your Baby's Heart Rate during Labor 141
  Accelerations in the Baby's Heart Rate 149
  Assessing Contractions 162
  Baseline
    Normal Range 110 to 160 BPM 143
  Decelerations in the Baby's Heart Rate 149
  Doctors Do Not Agree on Interpretation of Baby's Heart Rate 158
  Responding to Fetal Heart Rate Concerns 161
  The Concerning Fetal Heart Rate in Legal Baby Cases 159
  The Race Car Analogy 153
  Variability or Fluctuations in the Baseline 145
  What Is the Fetal Monitor Showing? 142
When Pitocin Should Be Decreased or Stopped
  Pro Tip 230
When Will They Stop Increasing Pitocin
  Pro Tip 227
Wrong Type of Fetal Monitor
  Tips for Your Labor and Delivery 187

Printed in Great Britain
by Amazon

129db92d-cdac-48b9-9f78-386fd0344c74R01